ALDENHAM SCHOOL

A Foundation for Success

ALDENHAM SCHOOL

A Foundation for Success

EDITOR: ROGER PAYNE

THIRD MILLENNIUM
PUBLISHING, LONDON

ALDENHAM SCHOOL: A FOUNDATION FOR SUCCESS

© Aldenham School and Third Millennium Publishing Limited

First published in 2011 by Third Millennium Publishing Limited, a subsidiary of Third Millennium Information Limited.

2–5 Benjamin Street

London

United Kingdom

EC1M 5QL

www.tmiltd.com

ISBN 978 1 906507 54 1

British Library Cataloguing in Publication Data

A CIP catalogue record for this book is available from the British Library.

Project edited by Susan Millership

Designed by Susan Pugsley

Production by Bonnie Murray

Reprographics by Studio Fasoli, Italy

Printed by Gorenjski Tisk, Slovenia

PICTURE ACKNOWLEDGEMENTS

Aldenham School and TMI would like to thank all the Old Boys and their families who have lent and given material so generously to the School Archive over the years. Most of the illustrations have come from the Archive. The School and the Publishers would like to thank Adam Scott for his superb modern photographs and also all those who have contributed images, including Marcus Blake for the archive images from 1913, Andrew Lewis, the Gillman family, Jonathan Simon, Walter White, Simon Boyd, Peter McDonald and Heather Sherman. The images on p57 appear courtesy of Alamy Picture Agency.

Every effort has been made to contact copyright holders but, if you have inadvertently been overlooked, Third Millennium Publishing would be very pleased to hear from you.

Contents

Editor's Acknowledgements

In 1998 Aldenham School celebrated its quatercentenary in grand style. The publication of this book is a further indication that we believe that in Aldenham School we have something to celebrate.

Aldenham School: A Foundation for Success is neither a traditional school history nor a register of former pupils. It is an attempt to convey not simply facts but flavour and to show that the success of the School depends at least as much on people and personalities as on achievements and awards. The first part of the book provides an historical summary with reminiscences of School life interlaced through the narrative. The last part is thematic and focuses on different aspects of School life with profiles of some of the individuals who have made the school what it is.

This book would not have been possible without the help and support of many people. I am grateful to James Fowler, Headmaster, for his vision in initiating this project, to the OA Society for their financial support which made the project viable, and to John Edwards OA for his work on the historical sections of the book. The bulk of the book, however, arises from those former pupils and teachers who responded to my invitation to provide reminiscences and to write articles, and it is they who have given the book its unique flavour. I have been hugely supported throughout by Heather Sherman, Marketing Manager, and by Molly Barton, Development Manager, and Jackie Wilkie in the OA Office. I am grateful to Susan Millership, Project Editor, for her patience and advice, and for her skill managing the whole process from inception to publication.

Inevitably, there will be disappointment that particular events and people have not been included, but difficult decisions had to be taken. Although every effort has been taken to check the accuracy of factual information, there may well be residual errors for which I can only apologise.

Roger Payne

Foreword

Each summer, the date for the Beer Money Ceremony appears in my diary and is quite correctly marked as a red letter day. This opportunity for all the pupils in Year 9 to visit the Brewers' Hall, to hear something of the history of their School, and to receive a ceremonial presentation of a coin from the Master of the Brewers' Company, is a vital part of their education. On that day, and hopefully on most days, as they are surrounded by the rich history of the School, they should feel that they are privileged to be part of such an institution.

I am always struck by the way in which OAs, whenever and wherever I meet them, are able to represent that sense of history so well. They will tell me realistically of the hardships of the past, but much more enthusiastically about the inspiring teachers who guided them, or friends who had sustained them through school and through life. And it is of course my role to listen and to understand what the School meant to them then and still means to them today.

I very much hope that this striking new book will convey not only that sense of the past, but also a little of how we are moving forward. When I speak to the new 11-year-old pupils on their first day in the School, I take only one book as a prompt which is the 1997 History of the School. This new volume will replace it, but the message will remain the same, which is that their aim during their time at Aldenham should be to realise the ambitions of Richard Platt, that they will advance in 'learninge, knowledge and virtue' and give thanks for that.

James Fowler
July 2011

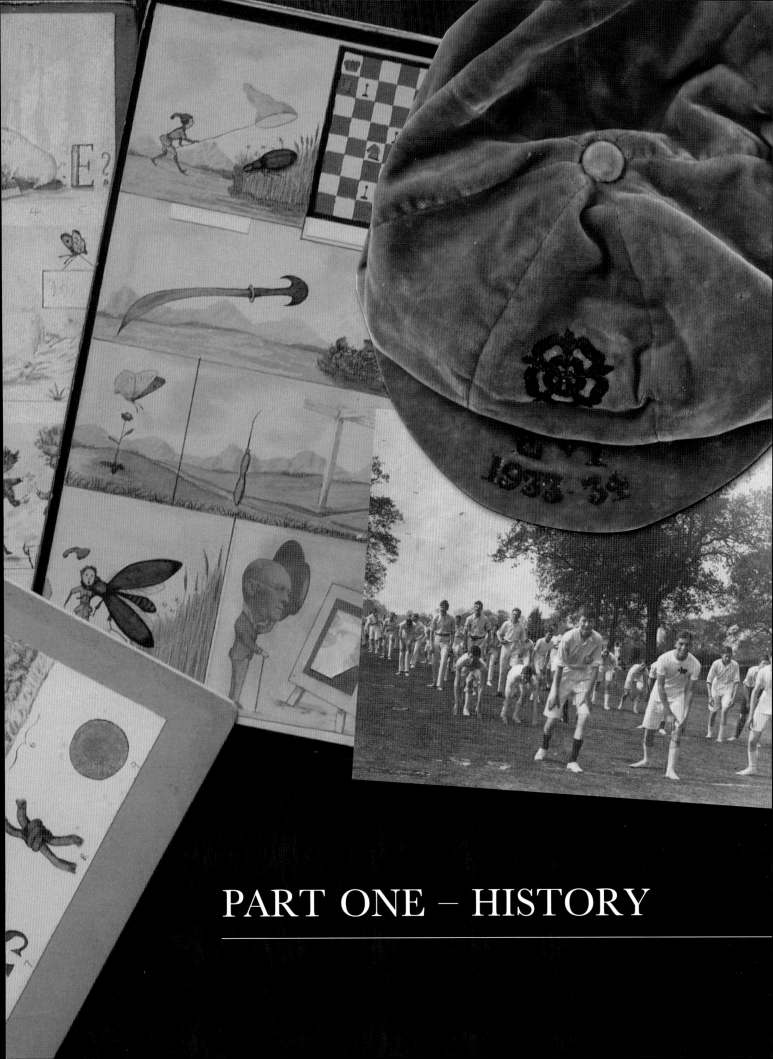

PART ONE – HISTORY

Beginnings: 1597–1899

In 1596, following the pattern established by other successful businessmen of the time, Richard Platt, Alderman, sometime Sheriff, and Brewer of London (1528–1600), obtained Letters Patent to establish a school. He chose his birthplace, the then remote Hertfordshire village of Aldenham. He started to build in 1597, which is the accepted date of the Foundation, although the first Master, Thomas Neale, was not appointed until 1599.

Platt chose the Brewers' Company, of which he had long been a member, as trustees. The Company obtained a Royal Charter in 1437 and in the 16th century it controlled all brewing within the City of London, then a heavily populated area. Members of the Company were the Governors of the School until 1873 and are still strongly represented. Individual brewers have been outstandingly generous to the School throughout its history.

Platt endowed the School with what was probably family land in the parish of Aldenham and a further 20 acres in the parish of St Pancras that was then in Middlesex. (This later proved a valuable source of finance when St Pancras Station was built on the site.) Platt conceived an academically strong school and went into great detail as to the character and functions of the Master and Usher and the curriculum to be followed, with considerable emphasis on the teaching of Latin. The School was to be free – for the sons of poor people of the parish and for the

Left: Portrait of Richard Platt aged 72, painted in 1600 by an unknown artist of the 'English School'. It hangs in the Dining Hall.

Right: Detail of the Original Charter.

sons of Freemen of the Brewers' Company; any spare places, up to a total roll of 60, could be filled from adjacent parishes. He emphasised the importance of religious observance and commended archery for pupils as being 'for the better exercising of their bodies'. He also founded almshouses close to the School, but these moved to Delrow in 1861.

Platt's mistake, which affected the development of the School until the 19th century, was to establish it in a parish that, between 1600 and 1825, had a population below 1,500. Most Tudor grammar schools were founded in towns: Platt had considered developing the former monastic foundation at St Albans and in the late 17th century the Company looked seriously at re-establishing the School in Watford. The low salaries offered and the relatively small endowment meant that, until 1825, one or other of the Master and the Usher was not up to the job and the School only achieved modest success as a rural elementary school concentrating on a purely English curriculum.

The Company made an annual Visitation and Neale, the Master, by then without an Usher, was dismissed in 1623 for incompetence; the low salary and the isolated position of the School made the posts difficult to fill even with the addition in some cases of a curacy and extra emoluments from the Company. St John's College, Cambridge found its task of presenting suitable candidates to the Company extremely difficult to fulfill, as the School's pupils were not educated sufficiently. Some stability was given by the appointment in 1650 of Edward Nicoll as Usher. He remained at Aldenham for 50 years, which remains a record. He was actually dismissed in 1670 because he was married, against

the requirements of Platt's statutes, but allowed to remain until a successor was found – 30 years later.

The Master in 1669, Andrew Campion, was invited to resign as the Visitation had commented on 'the fewness of the scholars and the non-proficiency of those that are there'. The Governors, in consultation with the people of Watford, discussed tabling a Bill to keep an elementary school at Aldenham to meet the actual local need and set up a grammar school in Watford. The idea was obstructed by Lord Holles, Lord of the Manor of Aldenham, who objected to the transference of money to Watford, and the Bill was consequently withdrawn. The subsequent history of the School could therefore have been very different. After the sale of the St Pancras lands in 1873, some money was transferred to Watford by the Charity Commission to establish boys' and girls' grammar schools, which now incorporate the Platt arms in their school badges.

An obvious remedy for the small numbers, the isolation of the School and the low salaries, would have been the recruitment of boarders but the Governors were reluctant to agree. Allen Allenson became Usher after Nicoll retired and was promoted Master in 1714. His son succeeded him.

A valuable survey of grammar schools in the 1670s by Christopher Wase includes Aldenham. He notes that the 'Master's stipend [then £20 a year] is usually below envy'. A Governors' Visitation about that time listed an inventory of the goods belonging to the School and the almshouses. There were 41 pupils on roll, all from Aldenham parish and all below the age of ten. Five bore the surname Nicoll, presumably the children of the long-serving Usher. The Schoolroom contained 'the ffounders effigies'

Left: Brewers' Hall. Until it was destroyed in the Second World War, this building was the headquarters of the Worshipful Company of Brewers.

Above: The Elizabethan 'Free' Grammar School. Completed in 1599 and demolished in 1825.

(perhaps the portrait which is still proudly displayed in the Dining Hall), 'ye Masters pew with a desk and lock and key, ye Ushers pew with a desk. One table and fframe with a form and Bench, 6 writing desks for ye Scholars, wainscot round and ye chimney piece'. Other rooms were listed including a chapel containing 'one door with lock and key, a desk with benches round, a large Bible and Common Prayer Book'. The Master occupied most of the building apart from a room above the kitchen for the Usher. There was a preoccupation with security and an inference of agricultural self-sufficiency reflecting the times and the isolation. The Visitors travelled from London on the improved road from Marble Arch (Tyburn to Edgware (of which the Company was Trustee). A meal was provided; that of 1671 cost a total of £1 5s 0d. The cost had risen to £18 6s 4d by 1815.

Allen Allenson, Master from 1714 to 1738, was more successful than his predecessors and raised the roll to 60. His son Gilbert attended the School and returned as Master when his father died, becoming the only OA to lead the School. Gilbert was an ordained minister and had two parishes but despite this got into financial difficulties and was dismissed in 1756, refusing to vacate the School until paid

£20, the equivalent of a year's salary. It was clear that the salaries being paid were increasingly inadequate.

In the years that followed salaries were increased, but there was no great improvement. Boarders were tried but left the Master in debt. Masters were often absent or parishioners complained of their drunkenness. It was very difficult to get a Master of Arts to take the appointment. In 1796 there were only 24 scholars and the building, the front of which had been shored up in 1772, was in very bad condition. In 1800 the Revd Methusalem Davies was appointed, with the limitation of pupils to 39, perhaps to allow him to take boarders.

Various factors led to an upturn in the School's fortunes; the Enclosure movement for instance led to the improvement of agricultural land and an increase in the local population. The Brewers' Company, in the Aldenham Enclosure Act of 1803, was allocated over 53 acres and the sum of £1,698 in 3 per cent annuities, which, carefully managed, significantly

Above: The Platt window in the Chapel, installed in 1999.

Right: Governors' Visitation Bill, 1671.

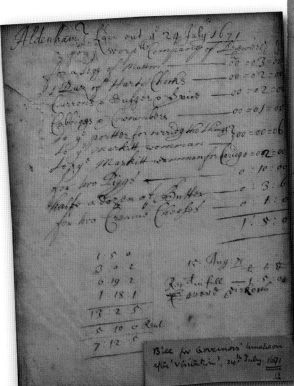

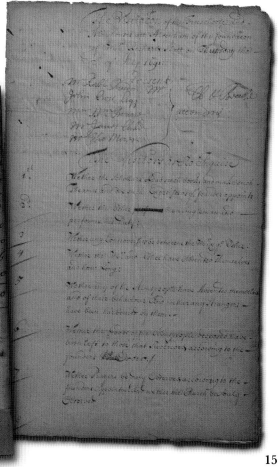

increased the available income. The growth of London also assisted as development reached the 20 acres with which Alderman Platt had endowed the School; the growing surplus income had reached £175 by 1800 and in 1807 was over £900. Davies was able to recruit some 28 boarders as well as 40 boys; he taught them 'the three Rs' and the rudiments of French and Latin. He was reputedly a fierce disciplinarian. The Governors were pleased with him, increasing his salary to £80 with £40 for the Usher, the stipulation being that the Bell Monitorial System should be employed whereby teachers instructed senior pupils who then passed on their knowledge, by means of questions and answers, to the younger pupils. The system was a failure in secondary schools and it was quietly dropped. Davies was teaching the boarders separately and was balancing the books, but the Governors felt that they had a duty to uphold the Founder's intentions and decided to dispense with his services. He became demoralised and ill, dying in 1823. The Usher, Summersby, took charge of the School, and Mrs Davies was treated generously by the Governors.

REBUILDING 1825–44

During its first two centuries, Aldenham had been a reasonably successful elementary school; some of its contemporaries had only ten pupils. In 1824 the Governors decided to create two schools, one a day elementary school or Lower School providing a basic education and the other a Grammar School, with a more challenging curriculum and many more boarders.

Plans for the Lower School included the building of a cottage for its Master. The existing building was to be restored with a new Schoolroom and two sleeping rooms on each of the two floors above. Thirty boys were to be Aldenham parishioners or the sons of Freemen of the Company, known as 'foundationers', while the Master could recruit 20 private pupils. His salary was raised to £200 a year while the Usher received £50. (A similar pattern was developed at other schools such as Rugby, Harrow and Tonbridge.)

Unfortunately, the new Lower School was shoddily built and by the early 1840s the buildings were collapsing. The first Master also collapsed, apparently driven mad by the noise generated by the Monitorial System, and was certified insane. The Newcastle Commission on charitable schools reported on the situation and the Lower School closed while two successor schools were set up at Delrow and Medburn in 1861.

Meanwhile Jonathan Wilkinson became Master of the Grammar School, at a salary of £200 a year. The building was found to be in a worse state than expected and it was completely rebuilt in a style that echoed its predecessor, the stone inscription above the door of the old building being placed over the door of the new. The building still survives, now used largely for administrative purposes, and the Tower, the School House

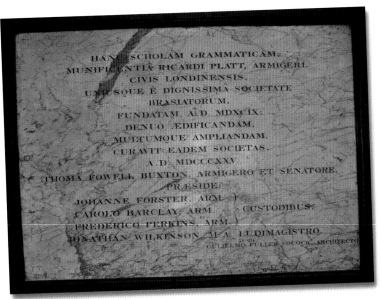

Left: The Games Shed was built in 1876 and demolished in 2005 to make way for the new Platt Building. It became redundant when the Sports Hall was built in 1992.

Below left: The Schoolroom was built in 1864 as an extension to the earlier building and was eventually incorporated into the refurbishment of School House, completed in 1992.

Cubitts, one of the great Victorian contractors, was paid £6,842 to build a Schoolroom capable of taking three forms to be taught simultaneously with two long dormitories above, linked to the 1825 building by a Tower which housed large water tanks to provide water for the enlarged School. A covered play shed, only recently demolished, was erected in 1876.

The curriculum was overwhelmingly classical; the highest class of seven boys, with the average age of 17 years and 6 months, spent 20 hours a week on Latin and Greek. A table of parental professions at this time indicates that boys were coming from all over the south of England from upper middle-class homes.

Leeman and the Governors argued over the future shape of the School. He believed that the small size, the limited nature of the entry and the paltry salaries paid to the teaching staff limited progress, although the annual reports on the School were very favourable. The Governors negotiated with the Taunton Commission. The Commission was committed to Aldenham being a public school, but money was deflected for other purposes: £20,000 went to the North London Collegiate School and Camden School for Girls, reflecting the St Pancras district where the increased income mainly arose; £13,333 went to the Watford Endowed Schools and £8,000 to the elementary schools at Delrow and Medburn which were part of the Platt Foundation.

Leeman was unhappy at the diversion of funds but it is possible that, had not the Commissioners realised the quality of Leeman's achievement, the sums diverted might have been greater. However the Commissioners, without a coherent plan, recognised that the endowments had grown through happy accident and were edging towards a national system of secondary education for girls as well as boys.

The governing body was reorganised by the Commission and now comprised eight members nominated by the Company, one by St John's College, Cambridge, two by the County MPs, one by the Hertfordshire County Council (after 1888) and two by the Board of Education. The Lord Lieutenant and the Chairman of Quarter Sessions were *ex officio* and two further members were co-opted. The terms Headmaster and Assistant Masters replaced those of Master and Ushers.

The release of funds led to better sanitation and better games facilities but Leeman, whose wife had died in 1871, had to some extent lost his zest; indiscipline among the boys had grown and the School was not as well respected in the neighbourhood as before. However, Leeman's contribution to Aldenham was immense: academic achievement was far greater, the quality of life of the boys had improved and the ethos of the School had been transformed. An interesting comment on his time at the School was made by Lord Buckmaster (Lord Chancellor 1915–6):

Stanley Owen Buckmaster

Stanley Owen Buckmaster, 1st Viscount Buckmaster, GCVO, PC, KC (1861–1934) was at Aldenham from 1870 to 1879. He was in the cricket and football elevens, and left with a Classical Scholarship for Christ Church, Oxford. He became a prominent British lawyer and Liberal politician. He was Lord Chancellor under Asquith between 1915 and 1916. His obituary notice from *The Times* concludes:

A notice of Lord Buckmaster would be incomplete if it did not take account of his two most outstanding characteristics, his ingenuousness and the sincere warmth of his affections. These two qualities made him a passionate advocate of any cause which he espoused. Sometimes those causes were hardly worthy of his strenuous advocacy or of the magnificent diction in which he clothed it. But they were the man.

We were a race with the vices and virtues of savages, proud of knowing nothing of personal cleanliness, to which we attached great importance, of speaking the truth at any risk, of strict honesty among ourselves, and of being able to drink more, swear harder and play football more violently than any other boys in the kingdom.

It is fortunate that other boys of this period have left a record of their time at Aldenham. DF de l'H Ranking (SH 1862–7), later a distinguished lawyer, described his acceptance as a pupil at Brewers' Hall and the journey to the School, being driven from Elstree by Amos Holmes who was a well known factotum to the School. He wrote down his first impressions in great detail: *The School Room was a long room with lozenged windows; near the door was a platform with a desk, long desks running down each side, behind them lockers which served as seats and also as receptacles for books and for all the hundred and one odds and ends which form a boy's treasures … The boys were not long in impressing on me that I was a new boy and as such must bear myself lowly and reverently to all my betters … As small boys we all regarded [the Headmaster] with affectionate awe; and whom, as we progressed up the School, we grew to love and admire.*

Probably he was not an ideal Headmaster: he was easy going and had too keen a sense of humour but … he was a sound scholar and a man of wide and varied reading. He was of middle height, powerfully built, with a red face and grizzled hair and whiskers, somewhat careless in his dress … he would administer instantaneous justice to any offending small boy.

Mrs Leeman was also much respected and, on medical advice, pu-r-r-rged boys thoroughly. Her deputy, Sal, who was also the Cook would stand no nonsense but had a heart of gold and found bread and cheese for boys who were really hungry.

I soon found that school life was one of order and discipline, governed by settled rules, mostly unwritten, any breach of which being visited by a punishment, well understood, in some cases one especially made to fit the crime … As the newest boy in the long dormitory … I [kept] cave if we were indulging in a pillow fight, doing trapeze acts on the beams that ran across the room or indulging in a supper at unholy hours on the arrival of hampers from home …

Our life was simple and hardy. The bell rang at 6am in the summer … half an hour was allowed for dressing … a roll call by one of the Sixth, late arrival was punished by a fine deducted from our Saturday pocket money. Fines could sometimes be remitted by a meritorious translation or a brilliant catch at cricket. Our meals were Spartan … Breakfast and tea were blocks of bread and milk … beer was brewed on the premises and was served in white earthenware mugs.

The washing arrangements in the dormitories were calculated to inculcate hardiness. The basins were filled with cold water overnight and remained until the morning; in cold winters we frequently found it frozen. Neglect of proper washing was severely discouraged … I cannot remember that hot water was ever supplied.

Our range of studies was limited, in my opinion greatly to our advantage. Latin, Greek

Above: A clock was added to the Tower in 1897. Shown here are the clock's mechanism and the three bells that were made in Clerkenwell. The Aldenhamian commented, 'The improvement in punctuality is a wonder to behold'.

Above: Cricket team from the 1890s.

Right: Cricket figurines presented to the School by ME Stoner (1913–6).

and Mathematics were the recognised subjects with French as a harmless recreation … French was taught by Monsieur Pont … I doubt whether he had much idea of teaching, certainly nobody dreamed of trying to learn anything. We had to work the thing out for ourselves, and if we failed to produce a satisfying result we paid the penalty. There was no foolish theory that corporal punishment was degrading … we learned to rely on ourselves and we learned how to learn.

Of the assistant masters, Mr Nixon was a first rate teacher of Maths … Mr McGill and Mr Roberts were certainly the favourite masters of my day; they threw themselves heart and soul, not only into the work but into all the interests of the School, and the games owed very much to Mr McGill.

Out of school hours we had to devise our own recreations; we had to rely on ourselves for everything. Lawn tennis had not been invented, we had no racket courts, the only Fives courts were usually occupied by the Fifth and Sixth, the share of the lower boys in the game being confined to fagging the balls. The recognised games were football and cricket. Football was supposed to be the Harrow game but it seems now to be a cross between Association and Rugby. The ball was round and was kicked under the bar but you might under certain conditions hold the ball and run with it. There was no collaring but straight and hard charging was imperative.

Cricket stood on a different footing; we were proud of our cricketing heroes … everything connected with the preparation of the ground generally and of the pitches for matches was done by ourselves.

We did not play with other schools, always with clubs. The Eleven went to these matches in tax carts under the guidance of the redoubtable Amos Holmes, a staunch supporter of the team, whose stentorian shouts when we were winning could be heard all over the field. Other boys used to walk to support the School. We got to think nothing of walking 20 miles to and from a match.

Swimming we could only practice in the summer, when at least once a week we went to the reservoir at Elstree. Apart from these recognised pursuits we all had our favourite hobbies; many were keen on natural history (which included fishing and poaching). Once a year we had theatricals in the Dining Hall. The actors were carefully selected and coached in their parts by the Sixth. Costumes and scenery were got from Simmonds of Covent Garden. There were two performances, the first for the villagers, the second for parents and friends of the boys. We usually had two pieces, a farce and one of the old-fashioned burlesques … There was no canteen, no tuckshop and no place where the smallest article of clothing could be bought. For tuck of all kinds we resorted to Mother Moth at Letchmore Heath. Paddy, an old man with a cart, used to bring apples and pears for sale, in winter nuts and oranges.

The last two Sundays of the half-year were known respectively as Unbutton One Sunday and Cock Hat Sunday. As we walked to church it was *de rigueur* to leave the bottom button of the waistcoat undone and on the second the hat must be worn over the right eye. Aldenham was essentially a manly School; I never remember a bad case of bullying …

Ranking left in 1867. Reginald White's account covering 1873–9 is

such as a walk to Elstree to change a postal order or to Watford to buy cigars and tobacco (all the senior boys smoked as a matter of course), cleaning footballs and boots and greasing them with mutton fat, surreptitious trips after dark to fetch cans of beer from the Three Horseshoes …

All four resident Masters were graduates of Cambridge … the mathematical instruction was of the highest class and well carried out. Open Scholarships at Oxford and Cambridge were secured by boys inspired by Masters other than the Headmaster.

There were long gaps between meals and the boys often felt hungry. We were all adept at the arts of foraging and scrounging. Pheasants', partridges' and moorhens' eggs were enjoyed and milk extracted illegally from any reluctant scholastic cow that could stand such an operation. We gathered mushrooms, blackberries, sloes, a noble pike from Munden water near Watford …

In 1876 the Headmaster was persuaded to retire with a pension. On the last night of his reign there were scenes of the most unseemly jubilation … amid a constant flow of strong ale the noise and din was simply terrific. Windows, ceilings and furniture smashed and crashed in all directions. A threat to summon the police was received with derision. As an aftermath we had a longer holiday than usual as the damage had to be repaired.

But better times were at hand. Mr John Kennedy was a very different type from his predecessor … I was much struck by his demeanour and his kindness to a youthful schoolboy. Young, active, a wonderful scholar as befitted the distinguished and learned family to which he belonged, and of a pleasant disposition, he soon endeared himself to all save a small minority of reactionary diehards … joining us in our games of cricket and football, he was at all times accessible and we soon regarded him as our friend.

Harold Tyler (1872–82) gives a similar impression: Just beyond the Dining Hall were the so-called lavatories. There was a stone trough with a tap, no soap … the WCs were beyond description and one wonders that there was not a serious epidemic … Once a week there were two small tin footpans … and the same water had to be used by all (one could never wash above the knees). The rest of one's body had to wait for the holidays. An old woman called Polly Creeper used to be in attendance and she examined the boys' heads.

a marked contrast. He arrived at the age of 11 with his older brother: We had already experienced the routine of two boarding schools before settling down at Aldenham. Much to my surprise the whole of the School did not assemble on the appointed day but came dribbling in twos and threes and it was quite a week before all were present. Nobody seemed to care …

After a very cursory examination I was allotted to the lowest form. I then proceeded to take stock of the place. The School stood in the midst of green fields, used indifferently as playing fields and cow pastures. A herd of half a dozen cows formed part of the establishment to supply milk for the boys and cream and butter for the Headmaster's table … before any games could be played a certain cleaning up by fags was necessary and it was no novelty for a dismayed scholar to receive a smack in the face from a football plentifully besmeared.

The boys possessed a wonderful flow of strong language … their knowledge of the world in general far surpassed my own experience and I, being adaptable by nature, soon acquired a species of toughness which in my opinion did us no harm and taught us to look after ourselves. There were no restrictions in matters of bounds and we could visit anywhere we wished.

The Sixth possessed the right of fagging … the fag nearest received his orders … of a varied nature

John Kennedy

Revd John Kennedy (1847–1931) was Headmaster of Aldenham 1877–99 and was largely responsible for the construction of the School as it is today. He was educated at Eton and King's College, Cambridge where he was a classical scholar of distinction. In her 2010 article in *Aldenhamiana*, Liz Merrick, Kennedy's granddaughter, writes:

When John arrived, Aldenham was considered a small grammar school with only 47 boys, the School House, a play shed, three Fives courts and nine acres of land. When he leaves, there are 175 boys, the size of School House is extended and holds 90 boys. His development plan had created two new boarding houses, a sanatorium, a chapel, new classrooms, a science laboratory, a gymnasium and two swimming pools set in over 20 acres of grounds. In the eyes of the outside world he left Aldenham a Public School. Others described him as a brilliant organiser, always aware of what was desirable, possible or imperative. It is not surprising that the Aldenham Register calls him the Second Founder.

Right: Swimming Pool, constructed by John Kennedy in the 1890s but filled in during the 1980s.

Boys generally sat in the School with their hats on. When not in School one could go where one liked, providing one did not meet the Headmaster. The latter knew few boys by name … boys seemed to be able to go into a public house at any time…

This state of things changed in 1876 when John Kennedy came … I believe that the School was really bad only during the early 1870s when the Headmaster was becoming old, as I have learnt from some OAs that in the 1860s the School was a good one.

JOHN KENNEDY: SECOND FOUNDER

John Kennedy built on the best of the Leeman inheritance. He was full of energy and his presence was felt immediately. FH Clark (1873–8) recalls him appealing to the boys to get rid of their reputation for bad language and then 'he galvanized the classes under him to work as they never had before'. Games remained important but with a considerable degree of informality and there was still time and freedom for the individual to follow his bent, especially in the understanding of the countryside. ART Winkley (1877–83) observed that there was no uniform but the Headmaster encouraged the wearing of black coats and these soon became 'the rule'. He also introduced straw hats with the blue and black ribbon. The rest of the time a dark blue cap of 'pork pie shape' made by the village tailor was worn.

Kennedy carefully reviewed the School's traditions, abolishing activities that could lead to disorder and clamping down on bullying. Boys, however senior, were caned for transgressions. He knew all the boys and OAs would write to him and be sure of a sympathetic answer.

FW Winckley (SH 1903–10) wrote of the other staff: *Mr McGill was already an institution; he was a great naturalist with a flair for writing things and I remember the arrival of the newly published book on earthworms by Darwin, which he allowed me to look at. He kept an aquarium in the Masters' Room. It was properly planted and cared for – a small eel was a great attraction. He had a collection of old mark books with humorous drawings in them by himself …*

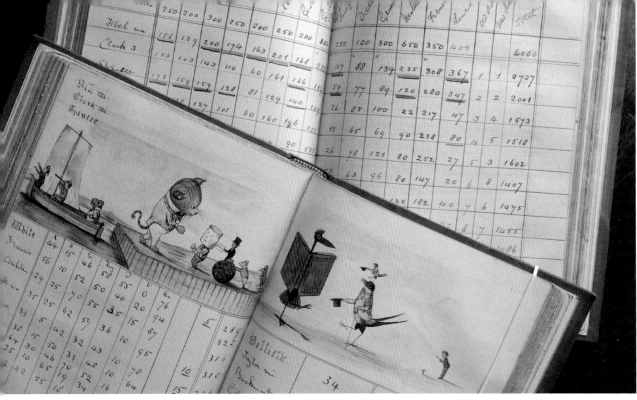

Mr Roberts was a kindly genial man. No one took him quite seriously although he would permit no liberties. His favourite recreation was to take a folding chair to the middle of Gravel Lane [Wards Lane] and there to smoke his pipe and read his paper. He wore a pea jacket like a sailor's in the winter and had a fine gold watch …

Of foreign language Masters the first I remember was Mr Oppen. He was an immense man, a Prussian, and affected rather startling attire: a blue coat with, I think brass buttons, white waistcoat, white duck trousers and straw hat. He was not unpopular – perhaps rather indolent. I remember seeing him with his head on the desk as if in slumber …

None of the Masters wore gowns, with the exception perhaps of the Headmaster. On Speech day however the Masters all appeared in the seediest of gowns. Mr McGill's was positively green with age.

In Leeman's final year the School obtained mains water supply. Before this all the water had to be pumped by hand from a well and this restricted the number of pupils the School could cater for. By 1897 Kennedy had increased numbers to 90 and the Governors agreed to build a second boarding house with Mr McGill as Housemaster. The stylish Dining Hall was erected at the same time.

That "Bülow" Feeling

Three generations of Aldenhamians

Before I entered Aldenham, my grandfather FW White (1885–91) told me a story of his time at Aldenham when he and his twin brother, my great uncle AF White (1885–91), decided in about 1890 that they should break up School early one term. They proceeded to home in Epsom where they arrived in time for breakfast, which was no small achievement in those days. They had arranged with another boy to answer for them at the morning roll call but unfortunately he muffed the requirements … The twins were severely reprimanded at the start of the following term. Their punishment was to leave School at the end of term at lunch time and not after breakfast. They found it a miserable experience, as there was no one else to play with. Needless to say they did not try to leave early again.

My grandfather was a keen sportsman and, unfortunately, a boy had won the under-14s 250 yards race three years running and so was permitted to keep the cup that had been in existence for some considerable time. The School accordingly provided a replacement solid silver cup dated 1887. Much to the School's chagrin, my grandfather proceeded to win the race on the next three occasions and was then able to keep the cup, which is now in my possession.

The twins were two of eight brothers that attended Aldenham. They had only one sister and she visited the School while they were there. She next visited some 70 years later when I was at Aldenham. She noted the many changes that had taken place since she had last been to School and wrote, unknown to me, to the Headmaster, PG Mason (1949–61). Her letter was printed in *The Aldenhamian*, where she referred to me as 'her nephew Theo'… A number of boys reached the article in question at about the same time and a cheer went up from the study block when my aunt Silvia's letter was seen. Congratulations were given to me for possibly being the first boy to have his Christian name in *The Aldenhamian* – a most improper occurrence of the time!

WTR White (B 1954–9)

TOPPING—*By Cumberworth*

AT VINCENT SQUARE YESTERDAY AFTERNOON WESTMINSTER SCHOOL PLAYED ALDENHAM SCHOOL A SOCCER MATCH — ONE SIDE OF THE GROUND — WAS LINED WITH WESTMINSTER TOPPERS

THE OTHER SIDE WITH ALDENHAM BOATERS.

THE REST OF THE AFTERNOON THE AIR WAS FILLED WITH BOATERS.

SHORTLY AFTER THE START WESTMINSTER SCORED — TOPPERS WERE UP; BUT

AFTER SUCH A VICTORY WE MAY EXPECT AN ELEVATED ALDENHAM BOATER

ALDENHAM WON 3 TO 2.

AND WESTMINSTER TO ADOPT THE DEPRESS-ED OR BISHOP'S LID.

By courtesy of the "News Chronicle."

In early January 1890, Kennedy resigned having accepted the headmastership of Tonbridge School. The Governors expressed 'deep regret ... at the loss the School was about to sustain and desired an expression of the high esteem in which they had always held Mr Kennedy and how conscious they felt of his exertions and labours on their behalf, which had resulted in raising the School to its present high state of efficiency and repair'. The post was advertised but Kennedy withdrew his acceptance of the Tonbridge headship and was promptly re-appointed at Aldenham. Albert Buckley (1889–93) gave a boy's-eye view of the saga: 'When we assembled for his last term, on the first night he came to read prayers as usual and to our bewilderment broke down completely. The same thing happened the following night, after which he made up his mind to ask to be excused the appointment – he just could not leave his School and his boys.'

Kennedy resumed his task with vigour. More classrooms were built, another boarding house (Beevor's) in 1895, a chapel (now the Music School) with stained glass windows by Edward Burne-Jones, many of which were installed in the present Chapel, a gymnasium and laboratories. A clock was added to the Tower in 1897 – *The Aldenhamian* commented that the 'improvement in punctuality was a wonder to behold'.

Mr WA Roberts was appointed in 1894 and was the first Aldenham Master to hold a science degree. Although the School had developed an excellent reputation for classical studies, Kennedy saw the importance of diversifying. Nevertheless three-quarters of a boy's time was spent on Latin and Greek with Maths a poor second. Great success was achieved. From 1877 to 1901, 57 scholarships and exhibitions were obtained at Cambridge; every

The Second Chapel (shown here) was constructed by John Kennedy in 1895 and converted to a Gymnasium when the Third Chapel was built in 1938. The First Chapel, built in 1884, of galvanised iron and thus known as the 'Tin Tub', became a museum.

Stained glass windows, made by the William Morris workshops to designs by Edward Burne-Jones, were installed in the Second Chapel. They included a memorial window to Alfred Leeman given by his pupils.

college being represented apart from Emmanuel and Downing, while eight were obtained at Oxford during the same period. At Cambridge the Porson and Davies University Scholarships, the Bell Scholarship (three times), the Abbott Scholarship (twice) the Latin Ode, the Porson Prize (three times), the Chancellor's Classical Medal and the Members' Prize for an English Essay were all awarded to Aldenhamians.

At the same time prowess in games increased. By 1900 the School had a reputation for football and had won 34 of the 42 School matches of which we have record. Good cricket was being played and some notable athletes being produced.

Kennedy was a first-rate organiser, holding a due balance between the School's material requirements on the one hand and its numerical, physical and intellectual advance on the other. His outstanding quality was his relationship with boys and the personal inspiration he gave them. Mr Beck, later Headmaster, who became a Master in 1893, gives a valuable insight: *Staff normally stayed until death or retirement. The curriculum was almost entirely classical. There were two Mathematics Masters and one Modern Languages Master. A visiting Music*

Master, father of the famous sculptor Alfred Gilbert, who was a pupil at the School, came down on Saturdays for lessons and choir practice. We were a bachelor community; ladies' society was represented by Miss McGill, who looked after her brother's house and often entertained us to tea.

The relations between boys and staff … were very happy. We had few interests outside the School. We had no bicycles, no lawn tennis courts and a great part of our spare time was spent with the boys … they expected us to turn out to bowl in the cricket nets and patiently endured our rough and ready methods of coaching. There was a free exchange of ideas between us and their loyalty and support were a precious bond of union.

John Kennedy was a teacher of unrivalled merit, a terror to slackers and evil doers, a cunning slow bowler and Fives player, a fine if dangerous fullback

Above: Old Boys Cricket Match, 1890. The top photograph shows the Old Boys team and the one below the School Team.

Above right: The Platt coat of arms in Aldenham Church.

at football …We knew our Headmaster well; every Sunday afternoon we trooped into his Dining Room to eat dessert and drink port, while in the evening we met him again for supper. What a teacher he was – ruthless in his demands for hard work and above all accuracy; untiring in his efforts to enliven the subjects he taught, caustic in his humour but ever ready to encourage honest endeavours – a whirlwind of a man. This is an inadequate description of one who ranks with the great Headmasters such as Thring of Uppingham or Arnold of Rugby … what he did for Aldenham can best be measured by the status he gave to the School which since its foundation had hardly been worthy of its Founder's generosity.

Part of Kennedy's success was the team he chose, made and inspired. HJ McGill, who had served 32 years retired in 1897. All contemporaries remember McGill for his characteristic shuffling gait, pleasant speaking voice, sweetness of character and temper, with power to command order through his own personality. Mr Paull wrote that 'He was so much beloved that questions of discipline did not arise'. He was a skilled naturalist, a capable and attractive speaker, and a man of exceptional generosity. Mr Beevor observed, 'He must have made a difference to the lives of very many boys, for he could see things through the eyes of a boy…'

Alongside the dedicated Masters was the key figure of Mary Anne Wiggins (1881–99), the Matron of School House. Miss Wiggins built up an unparalleled place in the affections of Aldenhamians. She had full responsibility for housekeeping and showed her skill in the care of both minor and severe ailments. Not always in good health herself, she put the needs of the boys first. The Revd GJT Harker (CR 1881–1923) remarked, 'One knew not which to wonder at most, the kindness and wisdom of her heart or her unfailing resourcefulness in every emergency'.

Kennedy had still a great deal to offer but Miss Wiggins was forced through illness to resign at the end of 1899 and this impending loss was the decisive factor in his decision to leave. The Governors accepted his resignation with deep regret and praised his 'invaluable services on their behalf and of his unselfish devotion to the interests of the School with the result that the School obtained its present high position and can compare most favourably with all other similar Foundations'. His influence for good and for high standards was to last for many years to come. The name of the School as Aldenham Grammar School had been dropped in the early 1890s and Kennedy had created a school that, though small, could in attainment rank with any Public School in the country.

Albert Buckley, later DSO and Bar and a Government Minister, wrote of his time at the School from 1889–93. He came from Liverpool, which indicates the national reputation of the School:

There were only six Masters besides the Headmaster … we had a drill sergeant called Fenner … there was a camaraderie between Masters and boys of the friendliest nature.

In summer we rose at 6.30am, worked from 7.00 to 8.00am, from 9.00am to 1.00pm, 4.00 to 6.00pm with prep from 7.30 to 8.30pm. Prayers were at 9.00pm and bed at 9.45pm. Latin absorbed never less than four hours a day. JK lived for the Classics and looked upon pioneers of what is now the 'modern' side as well-meaning and completely misguided …

There was little variety in the social life of the School … the standard of our football was high … we had a team that actually beat West Herts, then semi-professional, on their own ground. On Sunday we were called at 7.30am for prayers at 8am and breakfast immediately afterwards. Then there was Greek Testament and Church was at 11am. We arrayed ourselves in our best clothes with clean linen and underwear and trousers that had spent a week under the mattress. We all wore boiled shirts with Eton collars for the junior boys and stand-ups for the seniors …

Walking to Aldenham Church was an institution. You fixed your partner at the beginning of term and stuck to him to the end … Brothers walked together,

often the only time they spoke to each other during the week. All the local gentry went, as did most of the villagers. The high spot of the morning was the arrival by coach of Mr Gibbs' party from Aldenham House … They gave us a glimpse of the fashionable world. Lunch was always a cold meal … at four o'clock we had an hour's prep and from 5–5.30 wrote our letters home. Tea was at 6 and Chapel at 7… I learned chiefly through those Sundays at Aldenham to appreciate country life and picture the peaceful

Top: The School Orchestra c.1900.

Above: Boys at leisure, 1886.

Above and right: The Old Gymnasium built in 1895.

Right: Harold Gilbert (left), cousin of sculptor Alfred Gilbert, with classmate, 1880s.

village of Letchmore Heath with ... its atmosphere of quiet serenity. I never realised that the School was barely 13 miles from Marble Arch as the crow flies.

Buckley spoke warmly of Kennedy. He admired his erudition and fairness. 'Vigour was the keynote of his character' and he had no time for laziness or dullness. Beneath his tempestuous nature he had a very kind heart, spending time playing with the younger pupils and during epidemics he visited sick pupils daily, 'poking fun at those who were lightly afflicted but full of concern for those who were really ill'.

Buckley praised McGill, and CE Roberts who 'knew how to manage boys and stood no nonsense'. Roberts shared a room in the Headmaster's house with GJT Harker who taught maths. They apparently never spoke and divided the room in half with a chalk line. He remembers Johnny Goodfellow, the general factotum as: ... *the hardest working man ... he called us in the morning, rang the bell for prayers, took the shop, groomed the Headmaster's horses, attended to small repairs ... never idle, never tired ... It was a well deserved tribute to a faithful servant when in 1935 he was invited to open the modern School shop. Finally, I come to Miss Wiggins ... She understood Kennedy thoroughly. He always called her T and what she did not know about boys was not worth knowing ...*

Looking back on the educational value of his time at Aldenham he concludes that although the life and teaching was narrow, *it was not utilitarian; it aimed to produce scholars and gentlemen; it made us concentrate on our work ... it taught us to make the best of our brains. Most of Kennedy's boys have done well in life, some remarkably well.*

Five Generations of Aldenhamians

Dr William H Blake 1853–1933

William Twynam Blake
1881–1907
McGill's 1896–1900
Scholar of Caius College,
Cambridge
Died of peritonitis in India

Marcus Blake 1888–1933
McGill's 1901–5
Paymaster Cdr Royal Navy
Died of heart attack at sea

Philip Blake 1891–1962
McGill's 1904–8
Dental surgeon in Southsea, lived
in Havant
m **Marjorie Downs**

SISTER OF

John Philip Blake MC 1917–44
Paull's 1931–6
Captain of School,
Cambridge Blue
Scholar of St John's, Cambridge
Master at Sherborne
Hampshire County Cricket
Captain in Royal Marines
Killed in action in WWII in
Yugoslavia, 1944

David Eustace Blake 1925–
Paull's 1939–43
St John's, Cambridge
Dental surgeon in Southsea
Hampshire County Cricket

Charles Maurice Down
McGill's 1903–6
Croix de Guerre

John Maurice Down
Paull's 1935–9
Fleet Air Arm
Killed WWII, 1941

Michael Frederick Down
Paull's 1939–44
Captain of School
Pembroke, Cambridge

**Jonathan
Down**
McGill's
1968–71

**Charles
Down**
McGill's
1969–71

Christopher Blake 1892–1916
McGill's 1906–10 (below)
Read theology at Emmanuel
College, Cambridge
Died of wounds in WWI on first
day in France

Rhoda Blake 1897–1986
m **Charles Edward Wurtzburg MC**
McGill's 1905–10
Emmanuel College, Cambridge
Managing Director of Glen Line
Wrote definitive biography of
Sir Thomas Raffles

John Raymond Blake (right)
1898–1988
McGill's 1913–17
St John's, Cambridge
Injured WWI
Director of British American
Tobacco

Marcus William Blake
Paull's 1951–6
Dental surgeon
Royal Navy
Retired in Havant

Raymond Charles Wurtzburg
(far right) d 2007
Paull's 1939–43
Managing Director of
Mansfield & Co

Christopher Brian Wurtzburg
Paull's 1943–48
MA Cantab
Director of Royal Bank of Canada

chapter two

Changing times 1900–74

Dr AH Cooke, like his predecessor, was a product of Eton and King's College, Cambridge. He was an accomplished classicist and scientist. A man of wide and varied culture, he continued and expanded the Kennedy tradition. Aldenham was seen as a first-class classical school, with the science side developing. The majority of pupils aspired to go to Cambridge, where most of the Masters had been educated.

Left: The library as it is today.

Right: This late 1950s portrait of AH Cooke, Headmaster 1900–20, now hangs in the Dining Hall. It was painted from a photograph in the Hans Gallery, and subscribed for by OAs of Dr Cooke's time.

Cooke was Headmaster for 20 years but his most constructive time was prior to 1914. A third boarding house, Paull's, was opened in 1905. The momentum of Kennedy's work, maintained by the quality of the Assistant Masters whom he had appointed, continued. The Housemasters were all OAs and their solidarity as a group was remarkable, but Cooke took his place at their head with ease. The extra number of pupils raised the standard of work, allowing for a very necessary broadening and modernising of the curriculum.

Extra-curricular activities also widened. The Rifle Range was opened in 1902 and, so that Houses might compete more equally, School House, twice the size of the others, was divided into Odds and Evens. The Officers' Training Corps (OTC), later the Junior Training Corps and now the Combined Cadet Force, was set up in 1908.

Cooke was a staunch supporter of the OTC and Lieut. Col Wadmore and Sergeant-Major Hood

Left: Mr Paull's House. From a series of sketches by Leonard Patten.

Right: Caricatures of Masters c.1918 – Allsop, Paull, Gilbert, Beevor, Evans, English and Mead.

had untiring enthusiasm. Jock Evans, who succeeded Edmund Beevor as the School Historian, believed it contributed to the raising of standards of behaviour and tolerance of other people. It enabled many unlikely boys to cope well in the Services during wartime and during peacetime national service, and has enabled the successful careers of many distinguished Aldenham servicemen, including Lord Vincent, the last Field Marshal to be appointed. For a while the OTC went out of existence but now, in 2011, it flourishes again and has been granted Colours.

Two important Aldenham institutions started at this time. The Old Aldenhamian Society was set up in 1902 with Sir Samuel Wilks FRS as President and Edmund Beevor, who had produced the first edition of the School Register in 1898, as Secretary. It continues to give great support to the School as well as providing a forum where old memories and friendships can be rekindled.

Another important initiative, sadly no longer in existence, was the Aldenham Boys' Club in Kentish Town, near the area of the Founder's London Estate. A permanent clubhouse was opened at 93 Highgate Road in 1911 with 45 members and, the following summer, a party came from the Club to Aldenham as the first of many annual visits.

School activities continued to develop in the early 1900s. House competitions in every conceivable sport, as well as music and drama, flourished and in 1906 the School was invited to take part in the Arthur Dunn Cup. School games became compulsory but work was still regarded as an individual matter and there was not as yet an expectation that boys would pass examinations. GCF Mead (SH 1905–10), later a Housemaster, wrote that in the Sixth: *… we worked in our own time to a large extent. The result was that arriving at Cambridge it was just as easy to work (or not to work!) as it had been at Aldenham. There was no cramming for scholarships … we had definitely enjoyed our Classics at School … men from other schools had put in hours of work, which quite staggered us.*

Of his arrival at the School he notes: *I found that my chief duty all day was to spout i.e. to give translation of whatever book we were reading to the larger and tougher members of the Form. I liked doing this because I got treated at the Shop by the more generous of them …*

Sergeant-Major Hood

Frederick Hood was born in London in1877. Orphaned young, he enlisted in the army and served in India and South Africa. By 1902 he had moved to Letchmore Heath with his wife and was teaching musketry and boxing at Aldenham. Eventually he took over the School tuckshop but also ran the village shop selling newspapers, tobacco and confectionary.

At the start of the First World War Hood was instructed by the War Office to travel to Scotland to join the Black Watch Regiment. The Headmaster, Dr Cooke, immediately wrote to the War Office stating that if Mr Hood left Aldenham, the School's Officer Cadet Force would be disbanded. Mr Hood remained at Aldenham School and his descendants have a continuing association with the School.

Sergeant-Major Hood flanked by the NCOs of the OTC.

Certain exciting episodes stand out – how Willans dressed up as a mother and visited a Housemaster, claiming s/he had a son he wanted to send to the School and only failed to carry it off because he burst out laughing as he said goodbye at the front door; how Mead and Wurztburg bought a dog from a farm and surreptitiously fed it on School House food until it ran away; how Hartley played soccer for the County and then ran all the way back to School from the Watford ground because he had promised to play Fives after tea; how Duff pretended to have rabies … and managed to take in Matron completely for several hours …

RJ Evans felt that this Aldenham spirit was a great strength, often commented on by outsiders who only knew the School through its Old Boys. They were vigorous, direct, practical and highly principled, often immature compared with the products of other schools, but always likeable with a strong sense of loyalty – a clannishness that often resulted in school friendships lasting for life.

When Jock Evans came as an Assistant Master in 1916, the group of OA Housemasters made a great impression on him. Beevor, Paull and Gilbert were not so much brilliant schoolmasters but outstanding characters, yet very different despite having all been educated at the School and Cambridge, and then returning to Aldenham. (Evans never knew Mariette who died in 1914. He had taken over from McGill as Housemaster in 1898 and was a distinguished athlete and a scholar of Pembroke, Cambridge, who gave many generous gifts to the School.) Evans remembers Beevor, the son of a Norfolk squire, as being: *effective in everything he did, incapable of anything in the faintest degree mean or false or insincere …*

(cont. on p.40)

The First World War

One hundred and sixty three Old Aldenhamians and Masters gave their lives during the First World War. Many were very young, such as Christopher Blake, who died from wounds on his first day of action in France, aged 24. He had graduated with a theology degree from Cambridge. Eleven families suffered the double tragedy of losing two sons.

In May 2011 the School dedicated a plaque in St George's Memorial Church at Ypres, Belgium, to commemorate the members of the School community who died in the First World War and also those who have died in subsequent conflicts.

Dedication service in St George's Memorial Church, Ypres. Picture on bottom left shows Cyril Tyson (CR 1952–87) seated and President of the OA Society, Neil Sutherland (B 1966–70).

In grateful memory of the members of Aldenham School who gave their lives for their country in the Great War and subsequent conflicts

Charles James Shelley Dalbiac (B 1907–12), 2nd Lieut, 5th Fusiliers, was killed in action in Flanders, July 1915, aged 19.

Wilfred Armstrong Fox (SH 1906–12), 2nd Lieut, 4th Batt, Lincolnshire Regiment, was killed in action in Flanders, July 1915, aged 22.

Brian James Brett Walch (SH 1908–11), 2nd Lieut, 4th Essex Regiment, died of wounds in Gallipoli, October 1915, aged 21.

Maurice Richard Clift (SH 1911–5) was a member of the Cricket XI and captain of Football. In 1914 he gained an exhibition to Pembroke College, Cambridge but after receiving his commission in the Dorset Regiment left for France. He was wounded on 1 July and died in France on 4 August 1916. He had been wounded twice previously.

Second Lieutenant Harold Leslie Reading (SH 1911–6) served in the Royal Field Artillery. He was killed in action in the Ypres Salient on 5 November 1917, aged 19.

Lieut Colonel Henry Lex Francis Adam Gielgud (SH 1892–1900) was Head of the School and editor of *The Aldenhamian* in 1898. He went on to study Classics at Pembroke College, Cambridge and rowed for the University. He joined the Norfolk Regiment in 1914 and was awarded the MC in August 1916, after taking part in some of the heaviest fighting of the War on the Somme. Wounded on many occasions, he was killed in action on 30 November 1917.

1914 – 1919

MAIOREM HAC DILECTIONEM
NEMO HABET, UT ANIMAM SUAM
PONAT QUIS PRO AMICIS SUIS.
IOH. XIV. 13.

R.L.P.ADAMS	C.H. de WAEL
O.J.ADDYMAN	C.ELAM
G.A.ALLEN	M.FISHER
W.W.ASHCROFT	E.FITZ BROWN
J.ATTENBOROUGH	G.FITZ BROWN
G.H.BAILEY	W.W.FITZ GERALD
E.W.H.BARCLAY	C.P.FLEETWOOD
H.W.BARKER	C.L.FOSTER
W.H.BARKER	W.A.FOX
A.K.BARTON	T.FREDERICK
A.E.A.BECK	L.FULLER
J.P.BENINGFIELD	R.S.GASSON
F.A.BEWSHER	D.G.R.GEDDES
C.BLAKE	F.J.GEOGHEGAN
T.R.BLAND	H.L.F.A.GIELGUD
H.S.BLANE	A.S.GILBERT
G.W.BLATHWAYT	F.C.H.GILBERT
D.P.BONHAM	C.H.GIMINGHAM
R.M.N.BOURNER	H.M.GLEAVE
H.BOWMAN	F.G.GOODYEAR
H.J.BOWMAN	J.W.N.GORDON
J.E.BROAD	L.C.GRICE
R.G.S.BROWNING	H.J.HAMMOND
J.H.BRYSON	G.H.HASTINGS
A.R.S.CAMPBELL	A.H.HILLS
B.CARLETON-SMITH	L.G.HOLT
H.V.CHARLTON	W.P.HOLT
M.R.CLIFT	A.J.HOMERSHAM
H.L.CLOVER	E.C.HOUGHTON
W.H.COLLINSON	R.HOWELL
E.E.A.COLLISSON	C.J.HUNTER
A.W.H.COOKE	J.W.HUNTER
P.T.CROWTHER	A.H.HYAMS
D.E.CRUICKSHANK	M.C.C.JAMES
R.C.CUSACK	A.JAQUES
C.J.S.DALBIAC	E.C.JENKINS
G.H.DARBYSHIRE	B.JOHNSTON
J.R.DAVIES	P.H.JOHNSTON
C.J.J.K.DEAKIN	C.H.JONES
J.L.G.KEARTON	E.H.SALE
N.KEITH	G.B.SEWARD
C.H.M.KING	C.B.SEWELL
G.G.KNIGHTON	H.T.W.SHEPHERD
P.J.V.LAVARACK	J.E.C.SHIELD
W.E.LEGGOTT	W.SMITH
J.E.LUDLOW	W.L.SMITH
L.F.D.LUTYENS	A.G.STACEY
L.G.LUTYENS	N.S.STEWART
J.B.MAC BRAYNE	C.H.STOCK
B.J.MAC DOWEL	A.K.TARBET
F.D.MACKINNON	M.K.TARTE
J.E.C.MAC VICKER	G.C.TATE
P.L.MARMENT	P.C.TAYLOR
H.G.MATHIESON	J.E.TERRY
W.M.MEARNS	K.THOMAS
G.R.MIDDLETON	A.W.TOOVEY
P.T.MILLS	H.TOULMIN
F.M.MITCHELL	T.TOWNSEND
G.R.MONEY	F.K.J.TRAYES
G.MORTEN	W.D.M.TRIMMER
W.P.G.MYLREA	A.B.TYSON
G.ILE D.NEAL	S.W.UPCHER
J.D.NEILL	P.E.VINEY
B.J.NOLAN	B.J.B.WALCH
G.D.OCKENDEN	G.M.WALKER
B.B.PALMER	G.A.WARD
A.K.PARK	J.P.S.WEST
A.PARKER	A.WHITE-BOWMAN
J.W.E.PAUL	B.W.WILSON
H.P.PHILBY	G.WILSON
H.F.PITCAIRN	E.M.WINCH
A.R.POGGI	C.R.WINCKLEY
J.T.POLLOCK	L.H.WORSSAM
W.J.R.E.POOLE	F.O.WYATT
S.PRESTON	G.W.YOUNGMAN
H.R.PYBUS	
G.L.RANKING	
H.L.READING	
A.ROSCOE	
R.L.ROSCOE	
E.L.M.ROSE	
G.C.ROSE	
J.N.ROSTERN	
E.St.J.NORWOOD RYAN	
W.J.NORWOOD RYAN	

Teaching was only part of the day's work. After that came ... looking after his House, playing Fives with devastating skill, umpiring at cricket ... he took an active part in every department of School life ... he only flashed with real anger at things which he held to be below the level of an Aldenhamian and a gentleman ...

Beevor was largely the creator of the Old Aldenhamian Society. Mrs Beevor was a perfect complement to her husband. *She got the best from everybody all the time, because she always gave them everything she had and she had only the best to give.* Evans continues: *Paull's home was in Cornwall ... he had enough nervous energy to run several ordinary men. He threw himself with zeal into the exacting life of a Housemaster and nobody shared with such enthusiasm the doings of his boys. House matches were agonies and ecstasies. He could not bear to miss a match and yet it nearly killed him if his beloved boys lost ... There was a kind of fearful joy in French with JRP, rather like travelling fast in a car with worn tyres: you never knew when the bang was coming. Sooner or later somebody would break down; out would come the famous 'Tickle Toby', a short stick with a curved handle, justice would be done and the ordinary course of life would be resumed ...*

Left: HM Beck, Headmaster 1920–33.

GJT Harker remarked that during Paull's time 'there were no failures in Modern Languages'. By contrast, Gilbert came from London and many of his family had been Aldenhamians. He was tall, thin, precise, and Evans wrote that: *it was impossible to imagine him ever hot, untidy or excited ... he was an accomplished skater and fencer ... and could talk with distinction on a range of subjects which included old china, horsemanship, furniture and the social history of his time ... his discipline was strict and uncompromising, maintained with an entire absence of force ... Almost all his boys acquired something of his scrupulous honesty, his hatred of display ... One self-willed boy was shattered by his observation 'very well, you must go your own way ... you make me conscious of my failure and my inability to do anything to help you'.*

The mechanics of life at Aldenham had changed little; food, fuel and labour were plentiful and cheap; there was no running water in the dormitories, which Cooke toured at night with a candle, no telephone, no office staff, no transport and no radio. The journey to Radlett Station could be made by horse-drawn cart but most people walked.

During the First World War the School was hit by shortages of food, fuel and labour. Many young men left Aldenham to die in the trenches. Cooke's two sons served; one won a MC but his younger son, Alan (SH 1900–06), did not return. He was listed as missing and Evans recalls Cooke sitting in the hall waiting for the postman 'but the longed-for good news never came'. In his will, Cooke stated that 'his life at Eton, Cambridge and Aldenham had been continuously happy save for only one great sorrow' – the loss of his son.

Cooke resigned in 1920. Building on Kennedy's work he had, Evans considered, carried the School to the highest point in its history, 'all with such easy mastery and lack of fuss or strain that it was all taken for granted'. He was a great classical scholar and teacher. Mead wrote that, 'All his Sixth were expected to get scholarships and they always did'. Evans continued: *There can have been few men who disposed of their time so economically and efficiently. He did a full day's classical teaching as a matter of course. He never missed a match or a School function. He always took evening prayers and not a little later would be found sitting at the end of a bed surrounded by boys to whom he might be explaining where and how a mussel keeps its teeth.*

Right: The War Memorial Library opened by Lord Buckmaster in 1924.

Below right: The library as it was in the 1960s.

As a zoologist he had a Europe-wide reputation and gave talks to the School on a variety of subjects, illustrated by his own slides, which were the best they ever heard ... One of his secrets was his ability to concentrate only on what really mattered, which gave him enormous economy of effort. He ruled by suggestion.

Cooke died in 1934 after 14 years as Vicar of Mapledurham, Oxfordshire. In many ways Aldenham stood still during the next 30 years.

However, for the boys at the School, these were years of good teaching, solid pastoral support, notable games achievement and dedicated service. HM Beck, formerly an Assistant Master at the School, was Headmaster from 1920–33. Like the previous two Headmasters he was educated at Eton and King's College, Cambridge. On arrival he pressed the Governors to increase the fees, which enabled – with a generous legacy from Alfred Smith – the refurbishment of the School buildings, which had grown dilapidated during the war. New changing rooms, kitchens and servants' quarters were added, and electric light arrived in 1927 along with some central heating. The most prestigious and stylish new building was the War Memorial Library, opened in 1924 by Lord Buckmaster in the presence of John Kennedy, his old Headmaster. Under the guidance of CA Stott it became a model School Library, for which he received national recognition.

Beck started by overhauling the curriculum, the modernisation of which was the job of the Heads of Department, all young men appointed by Dr Cooke in his later years. Science teaching in particular made great strides; JM Wadmore (CR 1903–21) was the first Master with a science degree who had a real laboratory in which to work. He was an able chemist and tributes to his work by such pupils as Sir Wallace Akers, who was to become a Director of ICI

The nature of the School community was changing. The small, largely bachelor staff living in agreeable rural isolation, was replaced by a much larger group of 17 full-timers, many married. Some houses in Letchmore Heath were provided for married staff. Teaching was also becoming a better-paid profession with the adoption of the new Burnham Scales, while the Government Pension Scheme, transferable between schools, provided long-term security.

In 1923 'Bill' Harker, Chaplain and Senior Maths Master, retired after 42 years at the School. A lifelong bachelor he had a special place in the life of the School and his departure may be regarded as a watershed between the old type of Master and the new. Evans wrote of his 'polished' sermons 'infused with an idealism which many OAs of a different day gratefully remembered … Similarly his work in the classroom reached a high level of excellence and precision'. It says much for the enduring bond of the old bachelor community that he spent his retirement with his former colleague, Mr McGill, at Tunbridge Wells, greeting his colleagues still at work with a humorous letter at the beginning of each term.

Change was hastened by the coming of the motor car, which made wider excursions possible to London and other places of interest. It became easier for parents to visit their boarding sons and Aldenham became less of a national school but one serving increasingly its locality, especially the rapidly expanding population of North London and Hertfordshire.

Left above and below: The Third Chapel, built in 1938 by OA subscriptions and completed in 1958 by the generosity of two Governors, Col WH Whitbread and Mr JE Martineau.

Above: The New Classroom Block (now called the Maths Block) was built in 1933 with cloisters in front between School House and the Games Shed.

Ltd and Director of Atomic Energy Research, show how successfully the limitations of space, equipment and finance were overcome. W Green took over as Senior Science Master and successfully raised all three Science subjects to university scholarship level.

The national system of Higher and School Certificates helped teachers gear their work to the relevant syllabus, and the old 'go as you please' methods, inspirational though they could be, disappeared. The development in other subjects continued with Geography being introduced in a specially equipped classroom. In games the significant change was the levelling of the playing fields (now known as Cooke's Fields), much of which work was done by Masters and boys. Hockey was introduced and hard tennis courts built.

*Right: GA Riding,
Headmaster
1933–49.*

*Far right: A new
Tuckshop was built
as a uniform shop
and tearoom for
parents in 1933.*

*Below right: Break at
the old Tuckshop.*

Ramsay Dinnis (M 1926–30) spoke of the sparseness of the dormitories, the cold bath as soon as one woke up replaced by running across the Field to the swimming pool to do a length in the summer: *Every afternoon after lunch we either played organised games, levelled the future Cooke's Fields, split logs for the house fires or went for a cross-country run. Mr Gilbert kept a strict watch on all activities; he was very proud of the boys in his care.*

Beck retired in 1933, his headship marked by solid if unexciting progress. George Riding, his successor, came from the headship of Warwick School and who, like Beck, was not in Holy Orders but nonetheless a deeply religious man (the boys spoke of 'Methodist in his madness'). He helped to bring about the present Chapel of unusual design, completed after the war through the generosity of Colonel Whitbread, for many years Chairman of the Governing Body. An important sign of the times was the appointment of a Headmaster's Secretary.

A further prestigious building was erected at the time, an imposing classroom block between the School House and the Shed, and a tuckshop and uniform shop with a tearoom for visiting parents. Later, Basil Maddox (SH 1951–6) remembers the tuckshop as having three parts: *The counter (for cream buns, doughnuts and sweets), a tearoom, and a clothing shop which was an outlet for Gorringe's, the only designated store for school uniform. Clothing*

coupons were required, at least back in 1951. I never had money for buns, but each boy had a tuck box down in the 'chags' corridor with goodies from home. Cans of baked beans and stale cake were mailed to me by my mother. I saw her only once a term. We were always hungry of course, but slabs of bread and jam (no butter) were supplied after roll call, which occurred about five times a day, so we never starved.

And JM Helder (P 1945–50) recalls: *For someone who enjoyed their food, a visit to the tuckshop was a must most days. This was run by Mrs Timms, wife of our cricket coach, and when teasingly asked 'How much are the penny buns today, Mrs Timms?' she would good-naturedly reply 'Three ha'pence'. Tuesdays and Saturdays were highlights as fruit pies, which had to be ordered in advance, were a special treat to enjoy with a good friend.*

The main entrance was greatly improved by brick gateposts and wrought iron gates, the gift of Rupert Clift (SH 1914–7), who had returned to teach at the School (1922–37). He also provided a filter plant for the swimming pools and a squash court. His death following head injuries playing Fives was a tragic blow to the School. Bill Kennedy – son of John – who had returned to teach, wrote of him: *There was so much more he could and would have done; he bridged the gap between the traditions of the past and the new ideas of the future, he imparted a vigour of outlook and a charm of personality … Part of his substantial private income came from the considerable success, at home and overseas, of a selection of English verse which he and GCF Mead had jointly published.*

Shortly before the Second World War an option was placed on two hotels in Llandrindod Wells in Wales, as there was a fear that the School buildings might be requisitioned. In the event the School stayed put. Rooms used only or mainly at night were permanently blacked out with black paint or paper; no evening services were held in the Chapel. Everyone was issued with gas masks whose efficacy was established when a mobile gas chamber arrived. Underground concrete shelters were built for night or lesson time use; refuge trenches were dug on Cooke's Fields. There were constant practices. As there was a ban on bell ringing, the usual signals of School life were made by bugle calls. A night guard of two Masters and six boys was set up in liaison with the local Air Raid Wardens.

Alan Grieve (SH 1940–5) reflects on life at the School during the war: *Others will have recorded the*

School's limited exposure to incendiary bombs and the many hours spent rehearsing our fire drill. We also spent most of two, if not three summer holidays in farming camp, which was exceedingly hard work, but very pleasant. We slept under canvas, worked with horses rather than tractors, and gained first-hand and body experience of what farming involved. We did not wash much but there was a disused swimming pool, if I remember rightly … We were not totally relieved from farming after the harvest as we picked potatoes in the autumn, but, as one grew older in the School, working with the Women's Land Army had its attractions!*

Names were read out in Chapel of the School's casualties in the war and at the very end of the war I

Pupils taking part in farmwork: a makeshift dormitory at a farming summer camp during the First World War; planting crops at the School during the Second World War.

Neville Gillman

Neville Gillman (P 1931–5) joined the 4th County of London Yeomanry (CLY) in 1938. The regiment was sent to the Middle East in 1941 and Gillman was on active service from November 1941 until he was seriously wounded at the Battle of El Alamein on 25 October 1942. He commanded a troop of Crusader tanks in C squadron of the 4th CLY, which was part of the 7th Armoured Division's southern diversionary attack in the opening stages of the battle. Below is part of Neville's own, typically self-effacing account of his involvement in the battle which led to him being awarded the Military Cross.

We already had Monty's Order of the Day ... [we were the] first tank squadron through the minefield ... we followed a line of lamps across the January minefield into the gap between that one and the February minefield where we stayed all next day ... On the next night ... everything opened up on us from the flank and front; my searchlight and periscope were shot off inches from my head ... There were a lot of mines and a ring of anti-tank guns awaiting us and one by one my squadron went off the air stop ... as we started to move, everything opened up on us. The shell, an 88mm I think, came in one side and blew the other side of the turret wide open, killing all the crew except the driver and myself ... I felt a blow on my leg and fell into the bottom of the fighting compartment, and all the ammo was on fire, so I hauled myself out over the gun, out of the turret – I don't know how – and rolled off into the sand. My leg was broken in two places but the driver, Corporal Kennedy, hauled me away into a slit trench, dumped me in it and went off to find help. I sat there alone in the dark, feeling a bit isolated. I was taken back to an aid post, but the leg got gas gangrene and eventually had to come off.

Neville Gillman died aged 92 in 2010
Hon Treasurer OA Society 1936–93
Vice President OA Society

remember Derek Curling coming back to the School, having lost one of his lower legs and showing us how to use the slip catch in summer and to keep goal at football in the winter. We saw bombers limping back from raids in Germany and, I think, the gliders going over to Arnhem. Although not directly involved in the 1939–45 war, we were clearly touched and moved by it.

I remember that we were all actively involved in the Officer's Training Corps, as it was then called, or the Air Squadron ... The termly parade to Aldenham Church was a burden you either enjoyed or disliked ... On the subject of music, towards the end of the war, we did listen to the American Forces Network, and this, inconveniently, played the best music in which we were interested (such as Glenn Miller), round about the time we had to go to Chapel. This involved last-minute listening and fast catching up to get to Chapel on time!

Fortunately no bombs fell on the School, although there were many in the vicinity and the devastating effects in London lit up the southern sky. First Aid and stretcher parties were trained for each House and dressing stations designated, under the supervision of Dr Wilson, the School doctor (whose family were medical officers to the School for several generations) and Mrs Riding. The Junior Training Corps (as it now was) was especially active during the war, with close links to the local Home Guard. An Air Section and a Naval Section were formed. A key figure was Sergeant Major George Buckingham, an ex-Royal Marine who gave outstanding service, responsible for the Corps, swimming and PT. It was alleged that he sometimes got his roles confused, starting swimming races with the command 'Fall in'. He took the whole School for PT in the Yard, knowing everyone by name and holding everybody in thrall.

Sadly 113 OAs were killed during the war and many more wounded. The names of the dead are recorded in the Book of Remembrance and also on a brass plaque in the entrance to the Chapel.

In 1944 GCF Mead – boy, Master for 30 years, Secretary of the OA Society and Paull's successor as Housemaster – left the School. WH Kennedy wrote: *For 30 years he was completely identified with the School. Good discipline was assured by the natural charm of his personality, his enthusiasm for his subject and his efficiency. After a problem that had occurred, the Headmaster asked him to take over School Certificate supervision. On the day of the longest paper, English, he arrived each year with a bulky paper bag. At about half time he moved quietly round from desk to desk, probably 50–60 in number and on each he placed a bar of chocolate. It was a delight to see the faces of the candidates become suffused with pleasure and astonishment.*

Mr Riding retired to Cornwall in 1949. He had developed and extended Beck's changes in the curriculum, although it was still possible after the war for a boy to go through the School unscathed by science; Riding had a robust team of strong personalities among the Housemasters and assistant staff; he supported their commitment to their subjects and raised the whole standard of work and discipline. The School was moving forward although the war had inevitably prevented developments that might otherwise have occurred. Riding had tremendous energy; no task repelled him, however arduous, long or tiresome. He expected the same devotion in others and generally obtained it.

Leslie Manser VC

Flying Officer Leslie Thomas Manser (M 1936–8) was awarded the Victoria Cross for his bravery during the 1,000-bomber air raid on Cologne on 30 May 1942. The target was bombed successfully but his plane was damaged and taking heavy fire. Manser flew the stricken plane with great skill and ordered the crew to bale out. They urged him to follow but while the crew were descending to safety 'they saw the aircraft, still carrying their gallant captain, plunge to earth and burst into flames'.

Right: PG Mason,
Headmaster
1949–61.

Far right: The
Honours Boards,
which hung in the
Dining Hall until
the 1960s and
were photographed
before removal, show
something of the
academic achievemnets
of OAs in the late
19th and early
20th century.

ALDENHAM GRAMMAR SCHOOL
HONOUR LIST.

1877	H.J.CARTER	Scholar of Jesus College Cambridge.
	H.G.WINTER	Scholar of Corpus Christi College Cambridge.
1879	S.O.BUCKMASTER	Junior Student of Christ Church, Oxford.
1881	F.H.SIKES	Scholar of Pembroke College, Cambridge.
1883	F.H.J.TAYLER	Scholar of Magdalen College, Cambridge.
	J.C.CLARK	Scholar of Queens' College, Cambridge.
	H.H.COX	Exhibitioner of Exeter College, Oxford.
1884	A.F.B.CHURCH	Exhibitioner of Worcester College, Oxford.
	E.H.MARIETTE	Scholar of Pembroke College, Cambridge.
1885	H.C.STOKES	Scholar of Pembroke College, Cambridge.
	E.E.SIKES	Scholar of St Johns. College, Cambridge.
	H.E.GILBERT	Scholar of Caius College, Cambridge.
	E.BEEVOR	Scholar of Pembroke College, Cambridge.
	H.S.DISBROWE	Exhibitioner of Merton College, Oxford.
1886	H.A.THOMSON	Scholar of Pembroke College, Cambridge
	G.A.DAVIES	Minor Scholar of Trinity College, Cambridge.
1887	E.E.SIKES	Bell University Scholar, Cambridge.
	J.R.CORNAH	Scholar of Pembroke College, Cambridge.
	G.A.DAVIES	Foundation Scholar of Trinity College, Cambridge.
	P.O.ASHBY	Exhibitioner of Brasenose College, Oxford.
1888	E.J.P.ROSS-BARKER.	Hulme Exhibitioner of Brasenose College, Oxford.
	C.A.DAVIES	Porson University Scholar, Cambridge.
	C.R.LUZMORE	Scholar of Clare College, Cambridge.
	E.E.SIKES	Foundation Scholar of St Johns Coll. Cambridge.
	C.A.SILBERRAD.	Scholar of St Peter's College, Cambridge.
	M.SMITHER	Exhibitioner of Caius College, Cambridge.
	W.P.G.MYLREA.	Exhibitioner of Caius College, Cambridge.

ADJUSTMENT TO MODERN TIMES

When PG Mason became Head in 1949, Aldenham was more backward than most independent schools. Its ethos was old-fashioned, its physical provision poor. These reminiscences from Basil Maddox (SH 1951–6) capture the flavour of the School and the tremendous sway that Mason was to have over his life: *I was never Captain of the School, nor anyone special. Yet all I took away from Aldenham has shaped my life ever since. The knowledge, the experiences good and bad, the friends, the sports, so much packed into five short years … What intrigues me now is to realise the influence on my life, for better or worse, of one man, Headmaster Peter G Mason.*

As soon as I was born … my father immediately 'put me down' for Aldenham, where his brother, Dr Christopher Maddox OBE was an OA. Chris became much more famous than I did … At 13 I took the Common Entrance exam, and made a terrible mistake by scoring 92 per cent in both Latin papers, attracting the attention of PG Mason, who wrote to my father 'His line is definitely Classics. Please have him take Greek tuition during the summer'. I did. Ugh! The price I paid was to miss Chemistry entirely, which I regretted for the rest of my eventual career in Engineering!

The tuckshop reminds me of an incident that reflects P G Mason's attitude to sex. A boy who will remain nameless entertained his girlfriend to tea in the tuckshop on a Sunday afternoon while his parents, who had brought her with them, took a walk. PGM lectured him for that in front of the whole School in assembly. You'd have thought they were naked! The point is that we were sex-starved and living in a monastery – to hang up a calendar of a girl in a bathing suit was almost grounds for expulsion! To quote PGM, again during assembly, 'those pictures are just intended to give you a rise!' The only 'talent' around was PGM's own gorgeous blond German nanny Ruth, about whom many uncorroborated rumours circulated, all of them believed. Yes, girls were definitely off limits!

I cannot conclude without one more reference to Peter Mason. I disappointed him by abandoning Classics for Physics, and I will never know if the letters he wrote to Cambridge colleges on my behalf made the difference in getting me not one but two offers of places there. But I do know he tried, and I remember him kindly for that. The other Master I honour today was my House Tutor, Donald Parren.

An Art class in the 1960s.

I owe him so much, not least for my ability to write English, but much more besides! Masters see pupils come, grow and leave, and they may in time forget us. But we do not forget them … Five years is a small part of a lifetime, but they are the formative years. They were also some of the best, and I am grateful to have had them. Thank you Aldenham.

Mason had won the Porson Prize at Cambridge, the highest distinction in Classics, had a good war record and came from being Sixth Form Master at Rugby. He stayed at Aldenham for 12 years before becoming High Master of Manchester Grammar School, one of the leading academic schools in the country. He was convinced it was only the excellent schools that would survive. Emphasis was placed on encouraging boys to develop a more mature attitude to life and a greater sense of social responsibility. Maddox recalls two episodes that would surely have left Mason feeling despondent: *… we did have one annual dance. In 1954 it was held in School House Dining Hall, a night I will never forget. On a beautiful summer evening a busload of Sixth Form girls from St Helen's, Northwood, arrived. They were inspected before they came. Any suspected cleavage had to be concealed with a tucked-in scarf and lipstick was banned – but the girls told us they applied it on the bus anyway. And one young genius bribed the*

bus-driver to return an hour later than arranged. Unsuspecting, our chaperones marshalled us in the School yard on time at 10pm, then we waited, and waited … By the time the bus did arrive, after 11pm, PGM was frantically running all over the cricket field in the dark, shooing couples back to the yard.

…One awful moment in my last year, when I was a School prefect, I was shaken awake at 1am and told 'The Headmaster wants to see you in your study NOW!' Sleepily in my dressing gown I tottered down to my study to find PGM sitting in my chair. Open in the floor in front of him was a trapdoor, which had a 4ft crawlspace under it. The dusty bottles – wine, beer and spirits – were piled around my study, with many more still below. Hundreds of them. Obviously not all mine; some must have been 50 years old. But there was no way I could NOT know whose the full ones were… the Headmaster apparently expected me to rat on my friends! Sorry, no way! The School then had a problem. The Sixth Form boys run the School, so you can't send them ALL home! So the many real culprits didn't really suffer much …

Brian Apthorp (P 1951–6) describes some jinks that took place in the Sixth Form: *There was a fringe, almost lunatic group when I was in the Lower and Upper Sixth. Pylons were being built around the School, and soon dawn expeditions set out to*

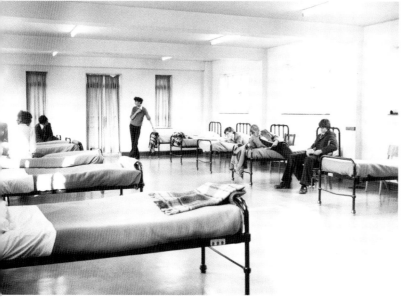

Kennedy's House was built in 1962 and named in honour of John Kennedy. David Wallace-Hadrill was its first Housemaster from 1962 to 1972.

to make the Music School. The teaching staff was provided with a much-improved Common Room. Studies were developed for senior boys. The Chapel was completed and Mr JE Martineau also presented two outstanding pictures by Stanley Spencer, whose sale in the 1990s saved the School from extinction. The most important building addition was a new boarding house for 60 boys, called after John Kennedy. It had studies for 25 boys with special recreation rooms and washrooms en suite.

The extra boys ensured that greater timetable flexibility and better facilities were possible. It also enabled the separation of the function of Headmaster from that of being Housemaster of a double house, however well served he might be by Senior Tutors of the calibre of Donald Parren, a talented teacher of English, and Jack Waddell, an OA and the respected editor of the School Register. A new house for the Headmaster was built, again through the generosity of the Brewers.

Sixth Forms were becoming increasingly more complex in the range of subjects parents expected the School to offer. Mason sought to delay early specialisation and added to the Sixth Form short courses such as science for non-scientists, history for the scientist, courses in art, music, current affairs and literature. Brian Apthorp further recalls: *The Headmaster Peter Mason was a Classics scholar, and he had the science Sixth Form doing a course in epic poetry, starting with Homer and going on through Virgil and even the Icelandic Sagas. This included Halgerda riding to 'The Thing', and one Norseman saying to another 'You load very little, and that you load badly' following which, in the saga, he took an axe and split the man's head so that his brains got mixed up with the fish in the boat. The Headmaster also had the classical Sixth doing a course on the meaning of science. He was really inspiring.*

As with her predecessor, Mrs Riding, Mrs Mason made a notable contribution to the School. The Masons' daughter gave the School the ultimate accolade by marrying an Aldenhamian.

Chris Wright taught at Aldenham from 1950 to 1967 and was the fifth Housemaster of Beevor's: … *When I took over Beevor's in 1956 I was immediately struck by the strangeness of our inheritance. The House even had its own language; boys were divided rigidly not only into year groups but into terms. If only one boy arrived in a particular term he was, strictly speaking, not allowed to talk to anyone*

climb them. They were known by mountain names *K4, Everest and so on. Although I did not take part I knew what was going on. Also Dupper Miller, in McGill's House, became something of a legend in explosives. With the aid of an alarm clock he could time an explosion – for instance to blow away a bit of guttering – so that it occurred during roll call, when the entire house was gathered together.*

The backlog of repairs had to be speeded up, the numbers in the School increased, new facilities provided and the general cultural life of the School enhanced. The science laboratories were improved, the Assembly Hall was gutted and refurbished to become the School Theatre and rooms were added

Left: The Tower, painted by Savory c.1925.

Above: School House garden as it is today.

without permission ... With the help of Bill Kennedy I reduced the isolation of the House, though it had one great advantage: it created that elusive and much derided bond, House spirit. This showed itself particularly in achievements in athletic standards and the House Music Competition ...

Helen [Wright's wife] still remembers the time she was shut in the bathroom bathing the two older children with one-year-old Hugh desperately crying for attention outside. The door handle had jammed and all she could do was to throw up the bathroom window and appeal for help from anyone who noticed her. The boys were in the Dining Room ... one of the Praes saw her and placed a ladder under the window. He climbed the ladder watched by a spellbound House; with typical Beevor's decorum he enquired whether he could be of any assistance. He was cheered as he climbed through the window. He was an expert clock repairer and quickly picked the lock, before withdrawing unobtrusively...

These days I often dream about Aldenham and its spacious and beautiful environment and I am almost always walking across the field from Beevor's to the Clock Tower or to Eros and the Common Room.

Fred English retired after 36 years at the School in 1951. Mason, whose Senior Master he was during the first two years of his Headship, wrote: *He was one of those generous personalities whom I had thought had died out when I was still at school. His achievements were remarkable. He taught French well, football better than anyone else; he played most games, always violently and often with success. You needed to be robust to stand up to Fred – what a small boy required was a sense of humour, some courage and a thick skin. He believed in the boys in his care and gave them strong encouragement. He saw teaching as the medium of a wider education.*

Michael Ridpath (SH 1940–4) recalls English's 'idiosyncratic' teaching manner: *Although I was more*

teachers, as Brian Apthorp recalls: *Mr Wright taught me how to reduce paragraphs whilst retaining their essential meaning. It was a most useful exercise and one for which I thank him even now … When I was in the Lower Sixth on a really cold day, 'Oily' Parren, the great English teacher, just before entering the class room started to recite 'St Agnes Ever, ah! Bitter chill it was…'*

In fact all the teachers were 'characters'. Griggs, who taught maths, had been in gunnery in the war. A student who had been doing some mathematical calculation assumed in his working that the gun went backwards at the same velocity that the shell went forward. Griggs wrote in red, 'Fool, where would the Royal Artillery be?' Mr Pollard was Head of Science and taught Biology and Botany, both subjects that I needed at A level if I was to pass the first MB … in the final exam, during the dissection my cockroach … disintegrated. However, I did not panic, and just asked for another one! Mr Harrington taught physics: he used to tell us to 'wrap a damp towel around the head' and learn formulae etc. which were to be written in a special note book entitled 'Everyman's bread and butter'. Chris Bolt, who taught chemistry, would appear in a tattered overcoat. I remember as if it were yesterday one occasion when he flung open the door from the prep room to the physics classroom and shouted 'Blaggard!' at Harrington, who continued teaching as if nothing had happened.

Most boys reached the Sixth Form and a good number seemed to slip effortlessly into Oxford and Cambridge. Basil Maddox was inspired by the School's long history and Oxbridge successes: *I can picture now the wood-panelled School House Dining Hall, with its dais and its inspirational gold-embossed honour boards listing those who had gained entry to Oxford or Cambridge, all presided over by the portrait of Richard Platt. It still amazes me that the founding of the School in 1597 was on this very site.*

Brian Apthorp tells a humorous tale of how his Persian friend helped choose his career: *Abol Zahir, who was in McGill's, became a good friend … It was in Abol's study, when consuming some caviar on toast that Abol asked me what I was going to do. 'Why not' said Abol, 'do medicine? Firstly you will not have to do National Service until you qualify, and then you will go in as an officer, and secondly you will not have to earn your living for at least five to six years. On top of that', he said, 'you are already doing science!' That was it; I got an introduction to*

than happy to be taught the French for Redstart, Wheatear and Nuthatch (all birds), I doubt it would have been much help in passing School Certificate or in day-to-day French conversation! He taught the language with a very broad brush. He tossed in some bits and pieces seemingly as they occurred to him as he went along, all of which he had us diligently write down in our exercise books. It resulted in something of a jumble, albeit of many gems.

Boys were made not to be idle, to play games, to take part in School plays and music competitions, as well as debates. Brian Apthorp was a keen participant in the newly formed Debating Society: *On the social side, I became a keen member of the Debating Society, and eventually its Secretary. I recall glancing though the minutes of previous debates to look for inspiration. One motion that had been debated in the past was 'In the opinion of this House, the noses of the poor should be reground'! Great stuff, but in the politically correct atmosphere that exists now, scarcely something that could be debated.*

Chapel had a major role and Aldenhamians were lusty singers. There was little indiscipline; most staff members were great characters as well as inspiring *the London Hospital via Harrington, whose cousin was John Ellis, the Dean, which must have helped at the interview, since I was offered a conditional place. Then I managed to pass at A level Physics, Chemistry, Botany and Zoology. The next stage of my life was about to start.*

English's successor as Senior Master was his great rival Jock Evans – their relationship was described as 'open enmity'. *The Aldenhamian* wrote: 'He had great interest in boys, persuasive charm of conversation, great efficiency in detail. Boys fell under the spell of his wondrous talk. His views on current affairs and on the world in general were always forthright and refreshing, stamped like bright coins in the mint of his own personality.'

Evans established Geography from scratch and made it a significant subject based on his comprehensive love of the countryside. He was also a keen historian and wrote the first history of the School. Cecil Stott, who succeeded Evans as Senior Master, taught at the School from 1924 to 1958. His great achievement was the School Library, which had 2,000 books when he took it over and 23,000 when he resigned, many acquired by him by scouring London to fill gaps. He did not believe in spoon-feeding; his aim was to show boys how to find out things for themselves. Basil Maddox fondly remembers encountering him on his first day: *I entered School House Evens at Easter in 1951, and my first memory was of being questioned by Mr Stott as to whether I was related to the Maddox whom he remembered had been at the School in the 1920s! Cecil Stott was a dear man; the School Library is a shrine to him.*

Peter Wingfield (P 1952–6) has similarly warm memories of Stott and his wife: *There was no room in Paull's House when I arrived with Alan Day and Michael Hobbs. We were drafted down to Stott's house, and were accommodated in a room upstairs. There were three beds, one of which we called the 'ditch' as it was more like a hammock than a bed. We would toss up for beds, and took it in turns to have the 'ditch'.*

We went up to Paull's House for breakfast and after prep in the Lower House room, we would go through to the private house where Mrs Pollard, wife of Pollard the Housemaster, gave us cocoa and biscuits and sent us on our way down the road to Letchmore Heath. I remember Mrs Stott bringing us raspberries from the garden. We were

very privileged to have been lodged out with such a kindly schoolmaster. He was always interested in our activities and interests in the School.

Another sad departure, in 1959, was Bill Kennedy who became Headmaster of Kirkham Grammar School. He had great ability as a teacher and was a talented games coach, an excellent Housemaster and never wanting in an emergency.

JM Helder (P 1945–50) was a keen sportsman who recalls Kennedy's great coaching skills: *I treasure my five years at Aldenham during the immediate post-war period, particularly for the wonderful playing fields. Not being academically inclined, sport was always a high priority with me so it's just as well in those days there were no girls at the School to distract me!*

Above top: This painting of Cecil Stott (CR 1924–67) by John Walton (B 1941–2) was the gift of the artist to the School and hangs in the Library.

Below: Letchmore Lodge was used as a boarding house for junior boys between 1955 and 1966 under the care of Raymond Griggs (CR 1944–71) and his wife.

I will always be thankful for the encouragement and coaching I received from that wonderful Master, WH (Bill) Kennedy. In 1950 there was only one position available in the First XI for a left back but even though I normally played at right half, Bill taught me how to play as a left back. At the end of the hockey term I was fortunate to be part of the hockey festival at Oxford University, where we played two matches a day for five days and in the evenings, if we were lucky, we were able to find a little liquid refreshment normally not obtainable at School!

Paul Griffin succeeded Mason in 1962, coming from the headship of the British School in Cyprus. He sums up the changing world that became the defining aspect of his time at Aldenham: *After the Second World War attitudes were very different*

Below: Beevor's cricketers 'posing' in the 1940s.

Bottom: School House cricketers 'posing' in the 1970s.

Bill Kennedy

William (Bill) Hall Kennedy (1912–2009) was the son of John Kennedy, Headmaster (1877–99) and taught at Aldenham from 1934 to 1959 where he was Senior History Master, Second Master and Fifth Housemaster of McGill's House. He had won scholarships both to Marlborough College and St John's College, Cambridge. He was a man of boundless energy and is remembered as an outstanding schoolmaster. In his obituary in *Aldenhamiana*, Bryan Robson (M 1949–53) writes:

No accumulation of tasks and responsibilities could weary Bill. In addition to housemastering, teaching, coaching, giving time to his family, he spent ten years as Secretary of the OA Society, which entailed meetings, dinners and a flow of correspondence. Resourcefully supported and balanced by Pauline's demanding work backstage, as well as her soothing presence among us, Bill's dominance of our McGill's community may be hard to imagine in these days of committees and management teams. It is only fair to say that if one pitched into the life of the House and did one's best for it, Bill's response was reciprocally warm. To me he was memorably indulgent and generous.

from those of today. Think, for example, of smoking, sex, discipline, dress, the Services, the Public Schools. We could have reached today's attitudes, good and bad, over many years; but the banked up frustrations of the young dictated a social revolution, and it came during the period when we were at Aldenham. Like many fast revolutions, it proved potentially disastrous, so much of our time had to be spent holding up the dam, and releasing change in driblets. Where change was needed, we tried to be helpful; where it was for the worse, there was bound to be a degree of conflict.

Peter Gough

Remembered by Paul Griffin, Headmaster 1962–74

Peter Gough came to Aldenham from Brighton in September 1966 to take over the Housemastership of School House and to teach Physics.

The Brighton legend was soon established at Aldenham. Before their first term began, Peter and Daphne, with much help from their three talented sons, had redesigned the interior of the private side … (Daphne's imaginative scheme for the redecoration and illumination of the Chapel interior was just as successful.)

…They loved entertaining, and no effort was too great: boys, staff, visitors and friends were all made welcome and enriched by sumptuous fare and hospitality that was both gracious and exuberant.

… In the House, Peter made his impact from the start (notably in House games, loudly spurring the least athletic to undiscovered competence and joie de vivre). He saw himself as a father to each boy, sharing with him both delight and disappointment: above all he was open and friendly … He hated having to speak harshly to anyone: his whole philosophy was based upon a Christian ethic of love …

He was so important a figure to Aldenham that it is hard to believe that he spent only eight years at the School. So much was crammed in, leaving so many dazzled and grateful parents, so much laughter, so much creativeness. He was a law unto himself, as was shown by my complete failure to persuade him to confine his spidery writing within the borders permitted on reports; but what a law his was!

Left: The School from Top Field.

Below left: Paul Griffin. Headmaster 1962–74.

Right: Jonathan Simon and friends.

Some change was easy: old 'traditions' about where to walk and whom to address were largely nonsense, which boys are sensible enough to recognise eventually. Parents also were prepared to abandon their romantic ideas of cold baths and beneficial imprisonment in favour of comfort, decency, care for others and, of course, employability.

Jonathan Simon's (SH 1963–7) recollections of his first few weeks show that School slang and curious traditions were going strong when Griffin arrived: *My parents and I arrived in the afternoon to have tea with the Headmaster in School House and meet the other parents with their equally nervous children. The next day was a big day with an almost military schedule. We were to go to the School and spend the morning meeting the House Captains, Praeposters, sundry other Sixth Formers and our 'guides' who would teach us about the School for the first two weeks. Soon we started to learn a code of curious rules for new boys and the rudiments of the School House dialect of the Aldenham language, which was like asking a barista for a cup of coffee, or asking an American waitress in a diner for eggs.*

The language used was English but the response was curiously unintelligible. There were two items on the schedules that were incomprehensible to me. In the middle of the morning and in the afternoon were two activities called 'Something'. I remember that I was very irritated by these items. How could a good school add such strange vagueness whilst orientating its new members? What kind of place could feature an activity that was indefinite and with no location? After two long hours of meetings with Sixth Formers, we were taken to the School House dining room and had something to eat and drink. Finally I knew what 'Something' was and was not surprised to have a cup of tea and cake in the afternoon.*

David Wallace-Hadrill, Chaplain, first Housemaster of Kennedy's, Second Master adds: *Every Housemaster got used to sitting up into the small hours with angry Sixth Formers demanding instant answers to big questions about the nature of human society, the purpose of education, the function of law and responsibility, and the right to self-determination. There were threats of invasion by motorcycle gangs and of arson to the School.*

Despite the turmoil, there was a 'silent majority' of boys who got on with their lives, working their way through adolescence, developing artistic or musical skills, passing examinations, playing competitive games. Griffin appointed four young Masters: Richard Jones, Chris Arkell (OA), Donald

Newton and Richard Wood – all of whom stayed at Aldenham until retirement and made a significant contribution. Games flourished with the football team winning the Arthur Dunn Cup in 1974. The School's sailing (on the Reservoir) was second to none and the School came third in the Ashburton Shield at Bisley. Aldenham was one of the smallest schools competing.

Griffin identified two major handicaps and set about overcoming them: *There was a desperate shortage of money and future bookings, and the establishment in our own parish of Haberdashers' Aske's School was a fiercely academic temptation to local parents. The money shortage could only be eased over a longish period by raising funds, a task in which our sponsors, the Brewers' Company, proved extremely generous. The competitive problem could only be tackled by being competitive ourselves. We chose Day Boarding, which gave local parents greater freedom, more weekend exeats for boarders that could be spent at home, and a Social Service Scheme, which partly replaced the less fashionable CCF, and put us well in touch with local people and institutions. We started an annual Prep Schools' Hockey Festival to keep us in touch with our traditional source of supply, and continued the good work when the Brewers came up with the money for a new Headmaster's residence ... Our numbers increased to a record 450, mostly boarders.*

In 1968 the School was the setting of the film *If*, which turned out to be quite different from the script Griffin had seen and approved. Fifty boys were employed as extras in the summer holidays; Arthur Lowe (an Aldenham parent) played the

Aldenham was one of the first schools to start team sailing in 1938. The Aldenham Team competing in the National Firefly Championships in Torquay, 1967.

Housemaster of a specially dirtied School House while his film wife wandered naked through the dormitories. The boys murdered the young and trendy Headmaster. In the film – in complete disregard of the producer's assurances – the Public Schools were mercilessly and hilariously sent up. The picture of Richard Platt was used without disguise. Beatings, CCF and discipline were all pilloried and some excessively unpleasant boys held up for sympathy and admiration. The film had a powerful influence for bad, not only at Aldenham.

Some concessions were necessary; the uniform was modified and a simple Sixth Form Common Room was built where beer was for sale, which was a financial success. It took the heat out of the problem of alcohol. Boys could now go home almost any weekend, which perhaps localised the School's clientele, but also meant that parents became used to visiting the School and watching games. Griffin remembers: *1970 was the Great Drug Year, drugs were freely for sale locally and I decided to force the matter into the open by confronting the senior boys and placing it in their hands and in a large and remarkable operation they cleared matters up themselves. A few already badly behaved boys had to leave, but the others who had merely experimented were able to make a fresh start.*

When Griffin retired in 1974 Wallace-Hadrill wrote: *... the fact that Aldenham stands today, unscarred and with a considerable reputation must in a large measure be due to the capacity of its Headmaster to keep cool at desperate moments and to make the community believe it was big enough in character to absorb changes without destroying its identity ... His quickness of mind was a sharp weapon and allowed him quickly to establish an authority and publicly present the School as a purposeful body which knew what it was about. He had great ability as a public speaker; he was not an easy man to work with, but not even those least in sympathy with him would deny that he was a man of consequence.*

Left: Brigadier John Platt presenting prizes at Visitation Day in the 1960s.

Below: Jim Robinson (CR 1974–85) with senior pupils in the Sixth Form Common Room.

Griffin gives generous credit to others for the successes of his tenure: *It was the quality and devotion of staff that made all this possible. If I have not mentioned names, it is because there would be so many. The same can be said for Governors.*

Jonathan Simon's observations echo Griffin's as he sums up all the things that he had acquired by the end of his time at Aldenham in 1967. He places great emphasis on the Masters and also mentions being guided through his teenage rebellion by Griffin:

I had:
- *a place at Medical School*
- *many good friends and wonderful memories*
- *an uneasy respect for the 'parabola' given to me by Mr Kirkwood*
- *a love of music and choral music given to me by Mr Hook*
- *an enjoyment of debating and acting that helped me with medical politics many years later*
- *a love of chemistry given to me by Ken Barnard*
- *an enjoyment of swimming given to me by Jack Waddell.*

I learned:
- *about humanity and tolerance from Dr David Wallace-Hadrill*
- *about current politics and disputation from RC Woods*
- *about the joys of British eccentricity and physics from Mr P Gough and started the Judo Club with his support*

- *about Biological Science from Mr SR Pollard*
- *about compositing and printing from Mike Davies*
- *how to use World War II radio transmitters*
- *to appreciate good photography by reading National Geographic in Room J whilst listening to pop music.*

I was:
- *guided through my 'If-like' teenage rebellion by Paul Griffin*
- *taught 'Pirates' by Sergeant Major EA Buckingham.*

I arrived with something in my mind and left with something else, broader and more important.

Some Eminent Old Aldenhamians

Arnold Duncan McNair, 1st Baron McNair (1885–1975; SH 1898–1902), a British legal scholar, university teacher and judge. From 1959 to 1965 he served as the first President of the European Court of Human Rights.

General Sir Richard Nelson 'Windy' Gale (1896 –1982; SH 1911–13), was awarded the Military Cross in 1918 whilst serving as a junior officer in the Machine Gun Corps. He eventually became Deputy Supreme Allied Commander Europe.

The Right Reverend Hewlett Thompson (1929–; B 1942–47) Bishop of Exeter from 1985 to 1999.

Field Marshal Richard Frederick Vincent, Baron Vincent of Coleshill (1931–; SH 1945–50), Chief of the Defence Staff from 1991 to 1992.

The Right Reverend Colin James (1926–2009; SH 1940–4), Bishop of Winchester from 1985 to 1995. He was a Vice-President of the OA Society and a former President.

Professor Sir Martin Sweeting OBE FRS (1951–; B 1964–70) pioneered small satellite technology and is the Director of the Surrey Space Centre.

Richard Frederick Vincent in front of the bust of 'Windy' Gale, 1997.

Arnold Duncan McNair.

Hewlett Thompson.

Colin James.

Martin Sweeting.

chapter three

The recent past: 1975 onwards

ON THE BRINK

In the last quarter of the 20th century many factors affected schools such as Aldenham. The Wilson Government was hostile to independent schools and abolished the hybrid Direct Grant status. There were also threats to charitable status and indeed in recent years the Charity Commission has weighed up the degree of public benefit. Rising inflation eroded investments on which many families might be relying to provide their children with a fee-paying education. Assisted Places, of which Aldenham had a small number, the purpose of which had been to enable children from poor homes to have wider opportunities, had been introduced by the Conservatives but abolished by the Blair Government. The Education Reform Act of 1988 dramatically increased central government control of the detail of education by introducing the National Curriculum, Standard Attainment Tests, the rigorous inspections of OFSTED and the introduction of League Tables. Although none of these were binding on independent schools they were, inevitably, yardsticks …

Peter Boorman came to the School as Headmaster in 1974 after several years as a Housemaster at King's, Canterbury. He felt his predecessor had left exhausted and was concerned that some of the staff

Opposite: Section from The Crucifixion *by Stanley Spencer.*

Right: Peter Boorman, Headmaster 1974–83.

In 1975 a new organ was installed and dedicated in the Chapel. Several distinguished organists gave concerts on the new organ in the years following its installation.

were obsessed by trivia. He feared that with the declining academic reputation of the School, it might become increasingly difficult to attract high-calibre staff, perhaps prejudging the School's continued membership of the Headmasters' Conference.

At once there were financial problems, a deficit of £42,000. Inflation was running at 20 per cent and the Houghton Award raised teachers' salaries by 33.3 per cent, backdated, for which no provision had been made. Boarding numbers were declining and it takes two day boys to compensate for one boarder lost in terms of revenue. To raise money, staff houses in the village were sold and cheaper accommodation created on the School site. Central catering was introduced.

In 1975 a new organ was installed in the Chapel through the generosity of Maurice Forsyth-Grant. A dedication and concert to inaugurate the new instrument was held in May 1975 and there were subsequent performances by distinguished organists, including Gillian Weir in 1976 and Allan Wicks in 1978.

There was a further Appeal in 1976, run 'in house' and raising £225,000, but unfortunately inflation and adverse adjustment of the tax-reclaiming arrangements for covenants reduced the effectiveness of the final yield. Hard play areas lit by arc lights were built and the pavilion refurbished. Most notably the Library was extended with a reading room upstairs and careers provision below.

Boorman was rightly proud of the success of the Appeal and he further improved finances by the creation of Camp Aldenham, a financial success that created considerable local goodwill.

Future numbers remained a worry. The Governors wanted to preserve the academic level and limit the number of day boys. Boorman, who had seen girls successfully introduced at Canterbury, wanted to bring them in. He was amused, perhaps irritated, by the Common Room preoccupation with what the girls should wear. To many of the staff the move was anathema. Separate accommodation in boys' Houses was designated, though Boorman now feels that one of the Houses, perhaps Kennedy's, should have been adapted for them. Girls were initially recruited into the Sixth Form.

Peter Boorman resigned in 1983 to take up another appointment. In 2010 he reflects on two of the major events of his time: *In my very first term, September 1974, I was invited to attend a two-day 'conference' at Wellington College along with other new Heads,*

Above: Sixth Form girls taking advantage of the new fitness facilities with Jan Chamberlain (CR 1982–2000).

Right: Sarah Schwepeke (B 2002–3) performing in the new Music School.

all relatively young with no training in Headship techniques, hoping to pick up a few pearls of wisdom from the experienced old hands, namely Frank Fisher (Wellington) and Roger Ellis (Marlborough). The first evening we sat round Frank Fisher's television hoping there would be an announcement from Lord Houghton concerning teachers' pay. We were aware that the news might not be included, being excluded by other more important matters. Far from being pushed out by other news, Lord Houghton's decisions were announced first. He awarded a 33.3 per cent increase in teachers' pay, backdated to the previous April! The TV was turned off. Roger looked pale-faced, Frank too. How on earth were we to face up to this really shattering news? We should also remember that other political matters, inflation and bank rate, were also looking grim. With commendable prescience the Governors had given me an extra 5 per cent in my budget for that year,

1974–5, in anticipation that a pay deal would have to be faced. When I returned to Aldenham with a very heavy heart, I knew that I would have to face the reality. We could NOT pay. My Bursar agreed. We put up the barricades and waited. Sure enough, what a fuss! One member of staff left me in my study, having slammed the door and said, 'You'll never be able to attract quality staff!'

The Appeal was planned and various 'specialists' were seen, with a view to getting one of them to organise everything. The final meeting at Brewers' Hall, attended by Sir Charles Hardie, Governor, and Jack Waddell and myself was memorable. Within five minutes of Craigmyle presenting their case as favourite bidder, Charles suddenly said, 'Right, we have heard enough. Thank you'. With that the three of us were left and Charles told Jack and me to get on with it. Jack and I stopped off at a London hostelry and before considering our plight had a drink or two. Jack was very good company!

The debate about full co-education at Aldenham School has a long history. It was seriously mooted in the 1960s, and reconsidered at various points along the way until its full implementation more than 40 years later. Sometimes the admission of girls throughout the School was rejected for financial and other practical reasons, but more often than not it was rejected because it was thought that such a move would change the nature of the School and its traditional ethos. The introduction of girls into the Sixth Form could therefore be seen as something of a

Jack Waddell

Jack was a mainstay at Aldenham for over 30 years, serving as an Assistant Master and throughout that time as House Tutor of School House Odds. He was Head of Classics from 1959 and responsible for many other activities throughout his long career at the School. Aldenham was Jack's life. He left Aldenham in 1985 and died in 1998.

After only two years at Aldenham, Jack became Joint Honorary Secretary of the OA Society. Following naturally on from this, in 1967 he became the editor of the Register Section of the 10th Edition of the Register and from 1979–82 masterminded the 11th Edition of the Register, notable for its articles on some outstanding former members of the Common Room and for many wonderful photographs of the School, old and new. It seemed inevitable that when the Governors decided to launch the 1977 Appeal without outside professional help, it was to Jack that they should turn to be Appeal Organiser. With his unique knowledge of OAs and parents, coupled with his immense capacity for letter writing, this Appeal exceeded its target. Among its lasting achievements are the Library Extension and the Redgra Hockey Pitch.

Alan Vening
Director of Music 1973–94
From The Aldenhamian

compromise. It would increase numbers in the School but without fundamentally changing it. Although numbers were small, individually, the girls enriched the School and many achieved notable success.

Caroline Frith (nee Spragg) (B 1982–4) was one of the first girls to join the Sixth Form at Aldenham and she recalls 'some happy and long-lasting memories': *My first experience of Aldenham was meeting Mr McAllister, the Housemaster of Beevor's. His friendliness, enthusiasm and above all his allegiance to Arsenal, made my decision to join the Sixth Form at Aldenham an easy one. In order to settle into the boarding school system, a new language had to be learnt. 'Call', 'something', 'Chapel' and 'prep' soon became everyday language for newcomers.*

The School employed a PE teacher, Mrs Chamberlain, specifically for the girls and despite losing our first netball match 43–0, sport for girls went from strength to strength. A group of us even completed the Eros Run, although we were unable to walk properly for several days afterwards. Due to the small number of girls, an 'X Factor' style of audition was not required for the choir and we were all duly selected by the memorable Mr Vening.

I studied French, English and History for my A levels. There was never a dull moment in our French lessons and I will always remember how appalled Mr Arkell was when, during the winter term, the girls began wearing leg warmers! Mr MacGregor taught English Literature with great passion, making Shakespeare come alive in the classroom. Mr McAllister's sense of humour always made History lessons entertaining…

Peter Boorman's successor was Michael Higginbottom, a Housemaster at Sherborne, a conscientious and deeply committed man whose principal thought was an understandable wish to be a hands-on schoolmaster, teaching as much as he could. He was first-rate with the pupils, but not so good at disciplining them or the staff who took advantage of his basic niceness. The hoped-for influx of girls did not fully materialise and, in retrospect, the signs were already there to indicate a relatively short life for the mixed Sixth Forms that so many HMC schools had enthusiastically embraced. Indeed by 1993 there were only ten girls in the School.

Above: In Church
by *Stanley Spencer.*

*Right: Portrait
of Michael
Higginbottom,
Headmaster
1983–94.*

*Far right: Stanley
Spencer working in
his studio.*

Higginbottom felt the management structures of the School had to be improved. The essential drive for change came from the new Chairman of Governors, Dr Tony Button. He had just retired as Chairman of Watneys and gave direct leadership working through the Headmaster and the new Director of Finance, David Billingham (an accountant with a senior background in GKN). Briefly the administration of the School was transformed. Both the finances and the assets of the School were properly and constructively managed, probably for the first time.

The School was £2m in debt with money from covenants barely covering the interest, and if this was to be reduced and improvements made, money could only come from the sale of the two Stanley Spencer paintings given to the School by Jack Martineau, Brewer and Governor. Much loved by generations of pupils, the sale was controversial but without it bankruptcy would have loomed.

Richard Wood (CR 1966–97) describes the Stanley Spencer paintings and something of their significance for the School: *The Stanley Spencer paintings, The Crucifixion and In Church, were given to the School by the Martineau family as part of the Chapel extension in 1958. Mrs Martineau was a great supporter of the artist. The two paintings offer startling counterpoints: In Church is a typical scene with the choir processing into the village church with friends and relatives in the congregation, whereas The Crucifixion is terrifying, with Christ being nailed to the cross.*

In 1993, *The Crucifixion* was replaced by *The Chapel Cross*. In an *Aldenhamian* article the sculptor, Juliette Anthony, describes how she set about the task of replacing this iconic painting: *It is not the easiest task in the world to replace a great picture like the Stanley Spencer Crucifixion. Of course, by the time I was asked by the Letchmore Trust to submit a maquette for their selection panel there was just a yawning space to be filled. It was 29 feet high by 17 feet wide by 7 feet deep (8.8 x 5 x 2 metres)! Having abandoned the idea of a sculpture rising from the floor or being fixed to the wall, I settled on a sculpture hanging from the ceiling. My thoughts then turned rapidly to the sculpture itself. Foremost in my mind was the mainly young audience that would be using the Chapel. I wanted my sculpture to have impact yet to remain simple, having a message not only for the committed Christian, but also for those of other religions and for those who are just not sure.*

The symbolic meaning of the outline of the Cross, the dove flying through the centre, the rays and nails slipping off the Cross suggesting the Resurrection must be obvious. For those who are in the Chapel looking for a quiet place to sort out a troubled mind, the dove is a symbol of peace whilst the nails remind us of the cruelty that was in the world at the time of Christ and which, unfortunately, is still very much part of the modern world.

Extending the age range of the School downwards to 11+ was an attractive proposition for Aldenham because, not only did it increase the total number of pupils in the School, but it also reduced the uncertainty in recruitment at 13+. In the early 1990s, it was agreed that entry at the age of 11 should begin as soon as possible and accommodation was upgraded both for boarders and for day pupils. A professional marketing manager was appointed. The business activities of the School were extended and a small Nursery School was created in the old sanatorium building. This was the most difficult decade in the history of the School. The seeds of the problems stretched back far before Higginbottom's time and many were external, quite beyond the School's control. The Governors seriously contemplated the possibility of closure and Dr Button's brief was to give it serious consideration. The Sports Hall, the construction of which had been committed to before money was available from the Appeal, had never been put into the accounts. Button was a hands-

The board behind the thief on the left of the picture is a segment of a beer barrel and the workmen hammering in the nails are wearing brewers' caps. Stanley Spencer told the boys 'I have given the men who are nailing Christ to the Cross – and making sure they do a good job of it – brewers' caps because it is your Governors, and you, who are still nailing Christ to the Cross'. It would be interesting to know what those present made of his speech. There were some people who expressed concerns about the suitability of The Crucifixion for a school chapel. Over the years, however, the paintings and the cartoons created a rich artistic heritage for pupils and staff.

The Crucifixion was sold in 1990 for £1.32m, the highest price at the time for a work by a modern British painter. In Church was sold a few years later. The cartoons are still in the school's possession.

David Wallace-Hadrill

The Revd Dr David Wallace-Hadrill was an eminent schoolmaster and respected theologian. He served the School as Chaplain from 1950 to 1955, as the First Housemaster of Kennedys 1962–72, as Second Master 1975–81, and finally as Librarian 1978–86. He left Aldenham in 1986 and died in 1999. Not long before his death, he wrote:

> We are most truly ourselves when we are least aware of ourselves in an act of creating. Time and space disappear and we are caught up for a moment into eternity. It is a kind of blissful annihilation of the self. But this experience of losing oneself – outside of time and space – is also what we mean by Death. Death is therefore to be welcomed as one welcomes the living creative moments of transcendence in our lives (when we are out of time and space and consciousness). Death is the completion and the realisation of the best that is in us. The end is not an eternal negation of our selves: it is the eternal concentration of our Being.

Richard Jones
Second Master 1962–94

on Chairman who positively managed the School, visiting regularly. The appointment of two Deputy Headmasters, Roger Payne and Richard Wood, both long established at the School, improved the management structure.

Michael Higginbottom retired in 1994. In 2010 he reflects on his experience of headmastership during those difficult years and on the crucial issue of 'numbers': *As any independent school headmaster will tell you, 'it is all about numbers' – of pupils that is. In little more than a decade, Aldenham pupil numbers went from 302 in September 1983 to 376 in 1989 and back to 324 in 1993. Reasons for both the rise and the fall are many, but include a general decline nationally in boarding and a more local reflection of economic conditions in North London, growth and prosperity through the 1980s and recession in the early 1990s. Aldenham in 1983 had already responded to the falling demand for boarding, especially at a distance from home, by introducing day pupils and encouraging weekly boarding. In 1983 there were 22 day boys and 30 weekly boarders (boys and Sixth Form girls), but essentially Aldenham was a traditional boarding school with a long school day and week, and with the House structure at its pastoral and*

educational heart. By 1994, 116 day boys were accommodated in School House (now Leeman's and Riding's) with a further 26 in the newly formed Martineau's (11- and 12-year-old boys), and 70 weekly boarders in the four boarding houses, leaving only 112 full boarders or just over a third of the total, but the full week and the House structure were maintained.

While not a conscious strategy at the time … Aldenham was moving gradually towards a distinctive niche in comparison to the predominance of large independent boarding and 'grammar'-type day schools in the area. Parents increasingly perceived the School as a different option, a small School with great pastoral strengths and well organised to enable pupils of average ability to fulfil their potential both academically and personally. Of course, this achievement depended as much on the quality and commitment of the staff as on the structure of the School. Aldenham at this time had a number of excellent teachers, and an especially strong group of Housemasters, who set the tone of the place and ensured a real community spirit, as well as supporting its Christian foundation and, implicitly at least, embracing Dean Inge's assertion that 'Education is the knowledge not of fact, but of values'. It is an overworked phrase that 'we shall not see their like again', but Aldenham certainly benefited over this period from teachers who demonstrated many of the virtues and very few of the vices of more traditional pedagogy: men like Michael Hetherington, Jack Waddell, Chris Arkell, Richard Jones, Richard Wood, Donald Newton and Alan Vening; and a younger generation including Nick Pulman, John McAllister, Austin Galvin and Bill Waite, and two excellent Chaplains, Peter Jackson and Simon Bloxam-Rose…

Stephen Borthwick, Deputy Head of Bishop's Stortford School, succeeded Michael Higginbottom. Tony Button, the Chairman of the Governors whose wisdom and energy was the key factor in averting closure, retired in 1995 and was succeeded by John Woodrow, the first OA to hold the office. Numbers continued to rise and the Junior School expanded. The School did well in an Inspection in 1996, which stated that pupils achieved at, or above, any reasonable expectation and particularly praising its sense of community, pupil relationships and preparation for adult life. The 1996 Appeal was a success and as a result, apart from general refurbishment, a new Artificial Turf Pitch, Music School and Technology Centre were built.

Stephen Borthwick left Aldenham School in 2000 to assume the headmastership of Epsom College. Aldenham was now a more confident community, keeping its traditional strengths and tackling problem areas with the improving finances. He reflects on his years as Headmaster as the School faces the future with more security and confidence: *In 1994, Aldenham was still struggling numerically with just 330 pupils, but the measure taken in 1992 to widen the intake to 11+ was key to optimism for the future. My feelings upon becoming Headmaster in 1994 was that the School had only narrowly avoided a major financial disaster by a combination of enormous efforts from a few senior figures, the wisdom of expanding the intake from 13 to 11, and the good fortune of clearing debt by realising the Spencer donation. All of this had been worsened by the recession, which was still with us in 1994.*

John Woodrow

John arrived as a pupil at this place, which he loved so much and which featured so strongly throughout his life, in 1946. He was appointed a Governor in 1989, not long before his retirement from Norton Rose in 1991. In 1995 he succeeded Tony Button as Chairman, and with Stephen Borthwick he worked very hard to raise the profile of the School and to bring it into a healthy position after what had been a difficult few years. He was the first non-Brewer, and the first OA to be Chairman. He was instrumental in the very important Quatercentenary celebrations and did some of his most vital work for the School as Appeal Director. What the Appeal achieved (a revitalised Design Technology Centre, the Artificial Turf Pitch, the Music School, the opening of Pre-Prep) was to put Aldenham well and truly back on the map both locally and farther afield.

...The level of detail of John's involvement with the School has been extraordinary. He was President of the OA Society from 1989–92, and Captain of the OAGS 1994–5. There is the Letchmore Trust and the Friends of Aldenham School, groups which contribute to and embellish the School and for whom John was a crucial player. His life and work was about people, and his contributions to these groups were always focused on how they could help others. All the time, he was giving back to the School that had meant so much to him. Through his work on the War Memorial and Jukes Funds, John was instrumental in helping to make a tangible difference to the lives of many pupils here. These funds helped parents in hard times to send or to keep their children at Aldenham. They may well never know who it was that helped them, but through his tremendous hard work for others, John's legacy lives on in this place in the form of lives transformed. There is hardly an aspect of this School that has not at some time seen John's hand gently but firmly guiding it, and every person living and working here, whether they know it or not owes much to his dedicated service.

John was a true gentleman, in the best Chaucerian sense of the word. His combination of humanity, courtesy and firmness perhaps sums up for me John's quintessential qualities. He had great charm and helpfulness, generosity, and a sense of humour and fun that permeated all he did. For John, diligence did not equal dourness – quite the reverse. He had, of course, that sharp legal mind that never missed a trick.

Richard Harman
Headmaster 2000–6
From a Memorial Service address

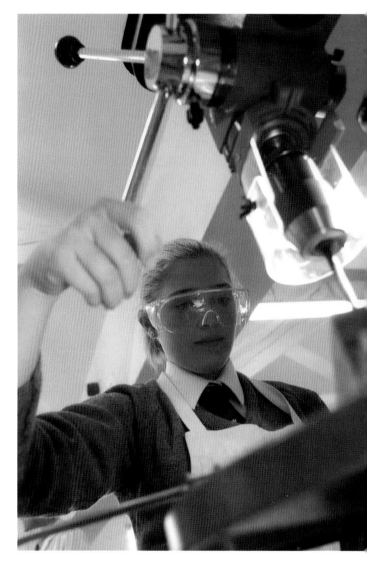

A major programme was introduced to improve the quality of teaching and learning within the School and in particular to introduce a scheme of 'whole-school' tutoring, whereby each and every pupil had a house-based tutor who did some group teaching but a great deal of monitoring of academic and extra-curricular progress. There was a need for more ambition academically within the School, and this required a greater sense of urgency. I had enormous help from my two Chairmen, firstly Dr Tony Button and latterly the late John Woodrow; equally important was the financial help from the Director of Finance David Billingham and later Andrew Fraser, my Bursar. This allowed us to set high financial targets and to be able to meet them in those early years.

There was much building work done in those early years with a new Technology Centre, a new Music School, a new network for IT and a lot of work

Above: Concert in the Waddell Recital Room of the new Music School.

Left: Aerial photograph of the School, 2006.

on boarding houses. Aldenham created a Nursery and was planning a pre-prep. In all this I was helped enormously first by Mr Richard Wood, my Deputy Head, and then by Mr Kevin Jones. Aldenham had a very encouraging HMC Inspection Report and pupil numbers began to rise, moving from 330 in 1994 to 410 in 2000.

The highlight of my time was the 400th anniversary of the foundation of the School in 1997, for which we produced a wonderful public concert in the Barbican Hall in London and a great time was had by all.

This concludes the historical summary largely written by John Edwards (B 1946–51), but this chapter would be incomplete without reference to some other major developments that took place in the 1990s and beyond, and to some of the people who made it all possible.

John McAllister (Beevor's Housemaster 1982–95) describes the impact of overseas students on the School and on the boys and girls concerned: *Over the last two decades, the independent sector has opened its doors to a wave of overseas students, initially from Hong Kong and China, and more recently from Japan, Russia, Korea and most significantly from Germany, and now Austria. As boarding declines in popularity, this influx has been the financial saviour of the boarding population, though to see it as an expedient would be*

to enormously underestimate the remarkably positive influence that these students have made to that most English of institutions – the boarding school. Most of the new wave of students entered Aldenham in the Lower Sixth, some for a term or two only, but many stayed to complete their A levels and often went on to study in UK universities.

Many of Aldenham's recent overseas students have performed to the highest level at Oxbridge and London Universities; they became leaders of House and School, and this is true of both boys and girls. They often excelled in the sports teams, notably hockey and football, and they made significant contributions to music, drama and even the Eros Run. Above all, whether they were successful or not, they have brought with them their own cultures and their own disciplines and they have been integrated into the ethos that gives Aldenham its individuality. Uncomplainingly, Aldenham's overseas students (averaging around 8 per cent of the Senior School numbers) have taken those challenges on board and have at the same time set an example to staff and pupils alike, which can only enrich the School community.

Keiko Takeda (nee Isobe) (B 2000–03) from Japan tells of her experience: *I enrolled as Aldenham's first Japanese girl student in 2000. I could read English with difficulty, but I was afraid to try and speak it in case no one understood me. It was a full*

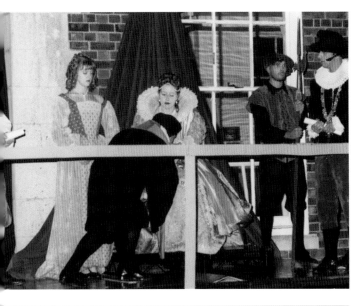

three months before I began to grasp what people were saying and another six months before I could respond with confidence.I was very lonely at first but my Housemaster, Mr Boothby, who also taught me Maths, was very kind and spoke carefully to help me. Also the Tutor responsible for overseas students, Mr McAllister, encouraged me to join in activities such as squash, playing the piano in a concert and I was delighted when he asked me to design the School Christmas card. I began to feel that I belonged … I will never regret joining Aldenham. By meeting new people and by experiencing new things in a different culture I gained the confidence to tackle many of the issues that face a student when they join the real world. Aldenham and its people gave me that confidence and I hope that one day,

my baby daughter, born in October 2010, will have the chance to study at Aldenham and to learn the lessons that I did.

The Quatercentenary celebrations in 1997–8 were major events in the history of the School and were designed to celebrate its success over the 400 years. Richard Wood (CR 1966–97), who together with Jane Britton (Marketing Director 1995–2001) organised the celebrations, describes the programme: *Aldenham celebrated its Quatercentenary in the academic year September 1997 to July 1998 and a series of events were held to mark the occasion. These commenced with a re-enactment of the presentation of the Charter by Elizabeth I to Richard Platt entitling him to found the School. The pageant was enacted in the schoolyard with accompanying music and refreshments, and it climaxed with a firework display on the playing fields. Fortunately the rain held off until the end of the festivities.*

Football was celebrated with a day of coaching for School sides by members of the Watford Football Club, a match between past and present stars of the Club and a combined School and OA XI, rounded off by a dinner to honour Donald Shearer, the captain of the first OA team to win the Arthur Dunn Cup, plus members of that side and also the second side that won it.

The OA Dinner was held at the House of Lords. The School Carol Service was held in St Alban's Abbey, allowing all parents and as many OAs who wished, to attend. The Abbey Eton Fives Tournament was held at the School and Aldenham won for the first time in five years.

Above: Music was provided by the Crissy Lee Big Band, Britain's only all-female Big Band, led by a teacher at the School, Crissy Lee.

Above left: Re-enactment of the presentation of the Charter by Elizabeth I to Richard Platt in 1597 entitling him to found the School.

Left: Stephen Boorthwick, Headmaster, buries a time capsule in the presence of the Chairmen of Governors, John Woodrow, two former Chairmen and two former Headmasters.

Right: A major highlight of the celebrations was the Spring Concert held at the Barbican Hall in London in March 1998.

Below left: Aldenham School Choral Society was joined by choirs from Dame Alice Owen's School, St Martin's School, Northwood, Lochinver House School and Northwood Prep School.

Below right: Aldenham School Orchestra was joined by staff, parents and friends of the School and was conducted by John Wyatt (Director of Music from 1994) and Geoffrey Barker (1965–99) Joint Head of Music (1994–9).

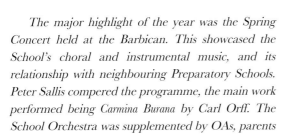

The major highlight of the year was the Spring Concert held at the Barbican. This showcased the School's choral and instrumental music, and its relationship with neighbouring Preparatory Schools. Peter Sallis compered the programme, the main work performed being *Carmina Burana* by Carl Orff. The School Orchestra was supplemented by OAs, parents and friends. It was a superb evening in memorable surroundings.

One of the 'fathers of rock climbing', the OA Archer Thomson, was celebrated by the School Climbing Club and OAs with a weekend in Snowdonia, during which several of the climbs he had pioneered were repeated using the clothes and gear of his period. This was followed in the summer holidays by a major expedition to the Dzhungarian Alps that straddle the Kazakhstan/China border.

OA Day in June was a family day featuring a Festival of the Car, a hot air balloon, planes, and the Band of the Royal Artillery, among a host of other activities. The day was thoroughly enjoyed by all who attended.

The year formally culminated on the 4th of July in a Grand Summer Ball, which proved to be a fitting finale to a wonderful programme of events.

The visit of HRH The Princess Royal in the autumn of 1998 was a bonus to the celebrations. Mark Boyd (K 1994–9), who escorted the princess on her tour of the School, recalls his feelings at the time: *I'll own up to having felt mildly apprehensive as an appropriately Royal-looking helicopter descended from blue skies on a perfect English day, to land on the playing field separating the McGill's and Beevor's boarding houses from the rest of the School. I was less nervous than I could well have been though, because the Matron of my own boarding house, Kennedy's, had rescued me from a sartorial catastrophe about 30 minutes beforehand! I was escorting the Princess Royal round and had some woefully creased suit trousers.*

HRH The Princess Royal was met, under whirring helicopter blades, by the Lord Mayor, the Chairman

of the Governors and the Headmaster, Stephen Borthwick. I was then introduced to her, and recall thinking she was very friendly, down to earth and unassuming. We embarked on a remarkably well-choreographed tour around the School. I'd decided my role was mainly that of opening doors, smiling permanently, and firing out the odd quip in a vain effort to be witty and charming; HRH seemed very gracious and amiable, despite the dubious success of such an approach...

The tour culminated in HRH giving a speech, and opening the new Astroturf pitch that had been built as a result of money raised by the Quatercentenary appeal. I then made a small speech in turn, thanking HRH for her visit.

In 2000 Stephen Borthwick was succeeded by Richard Harman, a former Housemaster of Eastbourne College, who writes: *I was fortunate at the*

Above and left: The climax of events in the autumn of 1998 was the visit of HRH The Princess Royal, who toured the school and opened the new artificial turf pitch.

Right: The new Prep School.

Below: Richard Harman, Headmaster 2000–6.

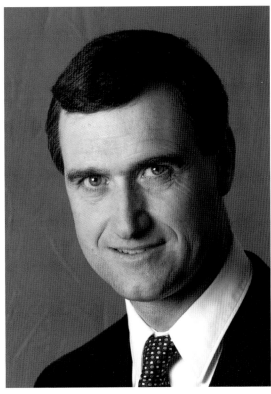

culture, and I quickly realised it was important to establish a new sense of direction and momentum.

The opening of the new Music School and the expansion of the Nursery into a Pre-prep Department provided excellent opportunities to promote the School and inject a renewed sense of optimism early on. Inevitably this also brought questions about 'Where next?' One of the most pressing priorities, which would also determine the future shape and size of the School, was whether to complete the 'bottom up' regeneration by filling in the education gap from age 7 to 11, in other words by opening a fully fledged Prep School. Once this question was answered in the affirmative, a number of other strategic decisions followed: the move towards full co-education; the expansion and reorganisation of the classroom and Common Room facilities at the heart of the main School (the Richard Platt Building also brought a sense of completion to the architecture at the centre of the School); the further shift away from full boarding and towards a day/flexi/weekly mix, though it would be left to my successor to end Saturday School; the growth in numbers and hence cash flow that all this entailed. In short, these six years were about securing the future of the School and providing clarity as to its direction and ethos in the new century.

All of this change took place in the context of my strong desire to maintain the focus on all-round development of the individual pupil and 'value added' as the cornerstone of an Aldenham education. This

dawn of a new millennium to inherit from Stephen Borthwick a School in sound financial shape and with considerable potential for further development. The difficult decisions he and the Governors had taken some years earlier had rescued the School at a perilous time. But they had also left some wounds for those who had been through a rapid change of

Left: The six Headmasters from 1949 to 2006 gathered in 2004 for the re-dedication of the replacement Headmasters' portraits, the originals of which were stolen in 2001.

Bernard Gordon

After a long career as a schoolmaster Bernard Gordon joined the staff of Aldenham in 1967 as Librarian and to teach some Maths. He left Aldenham in 1990 and died in 1995.

The boys to whom he taught Mathematics may not always have understood him, despite his beautiful lucidity of expression, but they loved being taught by him – they were fascinated by him. I was once able to tell Bernard that a very non-mathematical boy had asked if he could be transferred to the set taught by Bernard. I asked the boy why he wanted to be transferred. 'Well, sir', he said, 'I don't know what it is, but Mr Gordon seems to have gone right through to the other side and come back to tell us about it.' That was exactly the point; Bernard had seen the whole pattern 'on the other side' and the excitement and beauty of what he had seen had to be communicated to others, even the most innumerate … It is the old distinction between those who only see the back of a carpet with its apparent confusion of tied ends and those who see the patterns on the other side. Bernard saw the patterns and the tied ends and knots at the same time.

David Wallace-Hadrill
Chaplain, Second Master and Librarian
1950–5, 1962–86
From a Thanksgiving Service address

delicate balancing act would not have succeeded without the support of a dedicated team of staff, a hard-working and talented Senior Management Team and a committed set of Governors. However, John Woodrow's death, relatively early in my tenure, was a great blow. His personal involvement as Chairman is something I shall always be grateful for and cherish. A good working relationship between Chairman and Head is crucial to any school's success. In every future history of Aldenham I am sure that John's role in restoring the place he loved to full health will feature strongly. He worked selflessly and tirelessly, and contributed most generously, to ensure that Aldenham would thrive. I was delighted that, in tribute to John, we were able to name the Prep School building (developed on the Martineau's site) after him. It was truly moving to see John's widow, Daphne, unveil the plaque on which his name was inscribed…

Schools like Aldenham have been enriched by generations of men of character and flair who have given the profession variety and colour. They have been good teachers in the sense that they have conveyed something more than just subject matter to their pupils. They have also been good pedagogues and have efficiently prepared their charges for external examinations. In any case, they have stirred their pupils in ways that no exposure to teacher training could accomplish.

The profiles of Michael Hetherington, Jack Waddell, Bernard Gorden and David Wallace-Hadrill illustrate the quality of these Aldenham schoolmasters.

PART TWO – THEMES

chapter four

Continuity

In the late 1970s an informal survey amongst the teaching staff revealed a remarkable consensus about the historical strengths of Aldenham School. It went something like this: The School is located on an attractive, spacious and accessible site, close to good road, rail and air communications. It has extensive grounds, and is provided with some good buildings, facilities and equipment. It is a small and friendly place that enables boys to grow and mature with the encouragement and support that they need. It has a strong boarding tradition. Members of staff are able and committed, and they provide sound academic teaching and supervision of a range of other activities. Team games are played to a high standard. Clubs and societies flourish. The School has a strong Christian tradition and ethos.

Thirty years later those strengths are still acknowledged. The 2008 Independent Schools Inspectorate Report makes the following comment: *The quality of pastoral care and pupils' welfare is outstanding, successfully meeting the School's aims to nurture in pupils the character and skills with which to meet the challenges of life beyond School and within a small, caring community. The fostering of nurture prized by Aldenham's founder is clearly evident … Staff support and guidance for pupils is excellent, reinforced by a strong and influential house structure, which promotes genuine house spirit and a sense of belonging.*

It is a credit to all those involved that this thread of continuity still lies at the heart of the School. In many ways the School has changed in those intervening years as other sections of this book will

House Gaudy, 2010.

Common Room, 1993.

show but this chapter celebrates those things that have remained the same.

Those historic strengths are best illustrated in the experience of those who were pupils at the School and the reminiscences in this book testify to them.

Antony Wood (SH 1954–9) explains 'why it worked for me': *Thinking about the School day leads me to further thoughts about my schooling and why it worked for me. Gradually and very slowly at first, I began to do a few things well, acting, sport, debating, the Army Cadet Force etc. This in turn fed into my work, where I started to shine in History and English. Success at these 'wordy' subjects perhaps depends less on the retention of facts and more on argument and the use of words. And I was good at words. So Aldenham provided for me an upward, virtuous circle based on providing opportunities – have a go – some success – try something else. This seems to me to be as near the provision of an ideal educational system as we are likely to get. I was never 'brainy' or 'an intellect' but because of the confidence I got from doing other things well my work improved term on term. By the time I reached the Lower Sixth I was having a go at almost anything ...*

David Sweetnam (K 1976–81) claims that 'OAs continue to punch above their weight': *Luckily the five years flashed by, filled with sport, lessons, skiving*

and perhaps most importantly, learning to be self-sufficient and take responsibility ... Aldenham did indeed ultimately fulfil its mandate to prepare boys for adulthood, if not university. Perhaps, not least in providing constant opportunities to 'get involved', whether it be in a School play, on the sports field, or simply just being trusted to 'be in charge'... one can only help feeling that. This has to say something very positive for the 'old school'... I remain genuinely grateful for the enormous privilege offered to me during my time at Aldenham, which allowed me ultimately to undertake a deeply fulfilling career as an orthopaedic surgeon. Quite how I managed to end up as a doctor remains a daily mystery. However, perhaps one should never underestimate the ability of a school such as Aldenham to provide its pupils with the most valuable of all assets: self-confidence.

For many OAs it is the teachers who made the most lasting impressions, as Andrew Hunter (P 1972–7), now Headmaster of Merchiston Castle School, testifies: *To my mind, the key to the School at that time was the quality of many of the schoolmasters, such as Messrs Robertson, Jones, Hetherington, McAllister, Galvin, Arkell, Sadler, the Chaplain (Mr Dulley), Smith, Newton, Gough, Wood, Tyson, and, certainly from a pupil's point of view, the*

The Compleat Schoolmaster

If after 350 or so years Izaak Walton were to be reincarnated in order to write a companion volume to his famous classic *The Compleat Angler*, the model would be Michael Hetherington Hethers – *The Compleat Schoolmaster*.

First there were academic credentials that needed no questioning: University College School and St John's College, Cambridge, where he read Classics and became very knowledgeable about the Second Punic War of 218 BC. But this was no mere bookworm interest. After Cambridge he and several of his college contemporaries retraced Hannibal's route over the Alps with an elephant borrowed from Turin Zoo. An experience not to be forgotten, and obviously not by the elephant!

When he took up teaching, the gift that Hethers had in abundance was to be as deeply interested in the all-round development of each individual as in the subject matter of any particular lesson. The same was true on the games field. He himself seemed to excel effortlessly in every possible sport, regardless of the size or shape of the ball. But cricket was his greatest love and his prowess as a batsman impressed his colleagues on the staff. One of them did however once venture a doubt as to whether he had, as rumoured, scored 100 runs for the MCC on a particular date – or by that particular date!

This love of sport together with shrewd judgement of the potential of individual players made Hethers a formidable coach at every stage from Under 14 to First XI. Generations of Aldenhamians must look back on what he taught them about skills and tactics, dressed (if that is quite the word) in his trademark baggy shorts and red socks. Any of them who took him on at squash or Eton Fives at School, or at golf in his retirement, will remember that competitive grin after he had played the winning shot or sunk the winning putt. Glee without schadenfreude.

Apart from a year at a prep school in Kenya, Michael Hetherington spent his entire career at Aldenham, as indeed did a number of other leading figures in the Common Room. Any school would have thanked its lucky stars to enjoy the stability that came from having such a loyal and committed teaching staff. And Hethers, a supremely popular figure and highly respected Housemaster of McGill's, was at the very heart of it.

Arthur Hearnden
Common Room 1959–67

Headmasters, namely Mr Griffin and Mr Boorman … all these teachers (and many others), made an indelible impact upon me, whilst I did not necessarily think so at the time. As I re-read my School reports, there are gems of wisdom arisen from their pens, e.g. 'He works like a very able boy, and shoots from the edge of the circle like a good hockey player. He must be calm, though, when he misses.' And 'Though life has not always turned out fully as he desired, I hope that he will realise that to accept some shortcoming is part of the business of living. A marathon cannot be won at sprint speed.'

… At Aldenham, I was surrounded by teachers with presence and a lasting influence, and I now treasure the fond memories, the deep respect, and a lifelong growing consciousness of something taken for granted at the time. The teachers I have mentioned (simply because they taught me, were my Housemasters or Tutors, and coached me at sport) and so many others (whom I would not wish to offend by not mentioning by name) helped me to 'do and understand'. What's more, they have been a benchmark ever since in assessing my own performance in terms of how I try to inspire pupils and other teachers. However, I am going to give pride of place to Michael Hetherington and John McAllister amongst all the teachers who inspired me; they will know why! Whilst it was distressing, it was also a privilege to be able to speak at the Scottish Memorial Service for Michael Hetherington in Lossiemouth in September 2008 …

John McAllister (CR 1967–2005) recalls the impact of Michael Hetherington's disappearance: *The news of Michael Hetherington's disappearance whilst walking in the Drakensberg Mountains of South Africa at the start of February 2008 was simply incredible to many. Not only was he an extremely experienced walker, but, and more importantly, none of his legion of friends could possibly conceive of life without Michael.*

Seven months later nearly 500 friends packed into Aldenham School Chapel in a wonderful celebration of and tribute to Michael's life. The following week a similar service took place in Lossiemouth, Michael's adopted church, and once again the church was full.

SMALL SIZE AND STRONG SENSE OF COMMUNITY

Aldenham School has never had pretensions to be anything more than a small school where everyone knows and is known by everyone else. All those involved with the School understand the strength that comes from the intimacy that a small school provides. They also understand the strength that comes from the community spirit that is really only possible in such a school.

For Geoffrey Barker (CR 1965–99): *Aldenham's greatest strength is its comparatively small size, yet it has always offered the broadest form of education – academic, sporting and social. It has succeeded in moving with the times from the 'swinging sixties' through the technological revolution of more recent times.*

Because of the competition from nearby much larger schools, Aldenham had to offer something different, something special. In my view it did just that by holding its nerve and staying small. I always felt it really catered for and cared for the individual. I experienced this at first hand as a new member of staff in 1965, and I hope I practised the same philosophy towards everyone in my career at the School. *I can think of a number of individuals who might well have sunk without trace in a larger, less 'personal' environment.*

Within the School itself this small size had huge advantages. It was always the main contributor to the wonderful sense of being a community that the School achieved. We came together as a whole School (community) every day – Chapel services on weekdays and Sundays, and Assembly every Saturday. Although many of the Common Room lived in School houses in Letchmore Heath or on the campus, as the years passed, an increasing number lived out. This gave the sense of working in a broader community within the School and brought more of the local community into the School.

For me Aldenham was always part of an enlarged 'family' where, over time, I could get to know nearly everyone: not only the pupils and my colleagues in the Common Room, but the catering staff, the groundsmen, those who worked in the Bursary, the maintenance staff and so on – we all helped to make the place work. Members of the teaching staff were expected to contribute to the many activities that made up the 'whole-school' curriculum and I had the good fortune to be a part of the music,

Left: Kennedy's Games Room, 2007.

Right: McGill's House, 2008.

Far left:
John McAllister
(CR 1967–2005)
as Henry VIII at
the Tudor Banquet in
1992.

Left: Richard Payne
(B 1991–6) prepares
to summon guests to
the Banquet.

English and games departments, and over time to edit *The Aldenhamian*, to organise Friday Activities and Visitation Days. This gave me contact with almost every aspect of the School's life and its work force. I found it a constantly changing and invigorating environment.

For David Boothby (CR 1985–), 'a community needs a soul': *One of Aldenham's greatest strengths is that all learning, both in the classroom and elsewhere takes place within the context of a nurturing, caring community that lies at the heart of all that Aldenham is and does.*

That community of course consists of pupils and teachers but it is far larger than just that. Matrons, cleaners, porters, maintenance staff, gardeners, accountants, secretaries, catering and medical staff – the list could go on! These people all form a crucial part of daily life at Aldenham and without them the School could not function. They each fulfil a vital role in ensuring that the education of the pupils can take place effectively, but much more by their very presence do they contribute to the whole sense of caring, communal living that Aldenham offers. Aldenham is a microcosm of society, where each person has his or her own part to play in making the School *a community of caring individuals working together for the good of all. No pupil leaves without discovering the importance of treating all staff, be they teaching or domestic, medical or secretarial, ground staff or porter with courtesy and with gratitude.*

Living in the Aldenham community thus provides a unique and supported education in how to live in the wider society when a pupil finally leaves. The ability to get on with people from all walks of life, to interact meaningfully and courteously, to work together for the common good and to do so in a spirit of care and generosity is something that Aldenhamians can take with them from their School days. The effect of being educated in the community that is Aldenham can be judged not only by the friendly, caring atmosphere that is so frequently commented on by visitors, but also by the number of Aldenhamians who continue to return, maintain contact, support and in time send their own children to be educated at the School.

Pope John Paul II said 'A community needs a soul if it is to become a true home for human beings. You, the people must give it this soul.' The joy of the Aldenham community is that it is a home and it is given its unique soul by those who are part of it.

Above and right:
School House Games
Room in the 1960s
and more recently.

FLOURISHING HOUSE SYSTEM

It is difficult to exaggerate the importance of the House system at Aldenham. Other schools have similar systems, but there is something very distinctive about the way the system supports pupils at Aldenham. Sometimes systems overwhelm the very people they are designed to support. Not so here.

For John McAllister (Beevor's Housemaster 1982–95), 'Aldenham today flourishes because of its House system': *The House system is common to most schools; usually it is the first point of contact and for the next five years the House becomes a second home. Only a few decades ago, the primacy of the House at Aldenham was such that one particular Housemaster positively banned his charges from fraternisation with the neighbouring establishment and was even alleged, himself, to have refused to teach French to a young man who had decided against joining his House in preference for another. Such rivalry inevitably permeated amongst the members of the Houses and though there is no longer the bitterness of the past, there remains a healthy competitiveness that often stays with participants long after they have departed the alma mater.*

…But the sense of community and commitment that prevails within a House is not, at Aldenham, limited only to the inmates. For years, the parents have been increasingly involved in the educational process in its widest sense and the partnership between staff, parents and students is a priceless asset to this particular School. No longer are tearful teenagers delivered to the front door of the House in September to be collected *five years later by parents hoping that they will be able to approve the finished product. Today, it is a shared responsibility and it is a real testimony to the unique nature of the Aldenham Houses that social functions within the Aldenham catchment area are frequently transformed into Aldenham reunions.*

Today, Aldenham flourishes because of its House system. The sporting rivalries of the past continue unabated, the House Music Competition remains a calendar highlight and the sense of community and commitment are lessons for life. House traditions are maintained and new ones proudly created. Aldenhamians will often remember their Houses before their School and that is not necessarily a bad thing. Indeed the proof of the pudding lies in the experience of one eminent OA who was caught

Left: Paull's House.

Below: House Shield awarded to the overall Inter-House Competition winners; (bottom) the House Unison Cup.

short outside the Courts of Justice in which he was due to pass judgement that day. He was saved in his hour of need by a short-term but crucial loan of 10p from the lavatory attendant, who had felt inspired to make this philanthropic gesture because he had recognised that the eminent OA was wearing the same House tie as he was.

For Nick Pulman (Paull's Housemaster 1987–2002) 'the special community remains': *I joined Aldenham in September 1977 with two other young members of staff, one of whom handed in his notice on the very first day! Undaunted, I managed to find my feet teaching Geography amongst the gas taps of an abandoned chemistry lab, and working as a Tutor in School House, where a generous set of House Praes were happy to point me in the right directions – and later introduce me to my future wife!*

I was fortunate to have Richard and Gill Wood as proxy parents and such colleagues as Austin Galvin, John MacAllister and PK Smith, who could provide the necessary lighter moments. It was also of great benefit to sit and eat each evening and absorb the wisdom of Michael Hetherington and Donald Newton. My Head of Department was David Robertson who, apart from teaching me the basics of that game called hockey, was the greatest of companions on the numerous geographical walks that served as the Sunday entertainment for boarders at that time.

Charlotte and I entered Paull's in 1987 and were privileged to spend the next 15 years there. The House had many metamorphoses in our time, from mixed boarding, to all boy boarding and finally to a day house for Years 9 to 13, with Martineau's boarders (Years 7 and 8) doing the night shift! Some have asked how we went about ensuring that a day house ran with the same spirit as its boarding rivals, but it was reasonably straightforward. The boys (and girls) of Paull's never wanted to be second-best to Beevor's or Kennedy's so, with a little guidance, the momentum was always within the House ... and even day boys can sing (very well) in unison after six weeks of 'encouragement'! My only frustration within the time was that our gleaming silverware displays were dominated by hockey, cricket, athletics and music, but the main football trophies eluded us; until, that is, our final year when both Junior and Senior House were won on the same afternoon!

…Aldenham, like Paull's itself, is now very '21st century'. Technology and comfort abound, the fabric of the building is sound and the 'business' is secure – but the special community still remains, and I continue to enjoy working here. I am a day boy too, these days.

CHRISTIAN HERITAGE PROVIDING SOUND SPIRITUAL AND MORAL FOUNDATIONS

It is sometimes thought unwise for schools to celebrate their Christian heritage in the sceptical times within which we live. But Aldenham School is proud of the Christian values that underpin School life, values which incidentally are widely shared by those within the community who profess a different faith or none. The Chapel has been and continues to be at the centre of School life.

For some, like Charles Siu (B 1977–82), their experience of the spiritual life of the School was intensely personal: *Aldenham was the foundation of my spiritual life. I came as a doubter and a sceptic, but left with a profound faith. It was not as a result of hearing bible-bashing fire-and-brimstone sermons, but it was from the gentle warmth and fellowship of other Christians. Although I did not enter the ordained ministry of my peers, the same pastoral principles were used in my medical practice.*

For others, like Andrew Taylor (English-Speaking Union Scholar, P 1972–3), the impact was understandably different, but equally profound: *Albert Einstein said 'One cannot help but be in awe when he contemplates the mysteries of eternity, of life, of the marvellous structure of reality. It is enough if one tries merely to comprehend a little of this mystery every day. Never lose a holy curiosity.'*

At the age of 18, I spent a year at Aldenham on an English-Speaking Union scholarship. Having attended a secular school in the United States, I was curious to see how religion might feature in my new school.

…Having been brought up in the simple routines of a New England Congregational Church, I found the Anglican ritual, especially the frequent kneeling, burdensome. I could not bring myself to say the words, 'We are not worthy so much as to gather the crumbs from under your table,' words I deemed too submissive for a self-respecting Christian. No wonder my ancestors left England! Our School Chapel was dominated by a large oil painting behind the altar, depicting a violent Crucifixion scene. Christ was shown carrying the cross, not on Jerusalem's Via Dolorosa, but down a modern-day British street, being abused by the general public. (Art critics noted that the painter, Stanley Spencer,

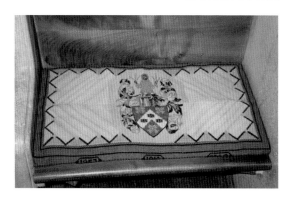

'*faced his doubts and dreads on canvas'. No kidding.)* The message to us schoolboys was: *You are part of that Christ-abusing crowd.* But, despite my early misgivings, I gradually relaxed my guard and found that the ritual, the music and – after I had absorbed its unsettling details – even the painting, actually helped my tumble-dryer mind to calm down and enter a different place, a place where it was possible to contemplate what Einstein calls '*the marvellous structure of reality*'.

My *Anglican UK School was serious about spiritual education, about nurturing students' souls in a way that my American secular school had not been. It helped me to grow in ways fundamental to my sense of who I was, and what the world, both seen and unseen, was about.*

For many Aldenham Headmasters, the Chapel was central to their work and they preached in it regularly. That did not change even when, from 1920, the Headmaster was no longer an ordained priest. When the construction of a new chapel was started in 1938, George Riding (GAR) was Headmaster. He was quite clear about its function: The unusual design of the Chapel was described by one of the Governors as looking like a power station (Battersea is its contemporary). 'That', said GAR, 'is what I intend it to be!'

More than a generation later, the Headmaster was equally clear about the role of the Chapel. David Wallace-Hadrill wrote of Paul Griffin who retired in 1974: *If any part of the School was central to him it was the Chapel, which he saw very much as being his own proper sphere of action and perhaps the most important manifestation of his own vision of what we were all doing at Aldenham.*

Chaplains too had their individual perspectives. The Revd Andrew Stead (Chaplain 1994–2004) writes: *In the ten years that I was privileged to serve as Chaplain I believed that the work of the Chapel was to be a point of access into the spiritual realm; that faith, and in particular the Christian faith, was actively lived and proclaimed and that it* was all taken seriously. I was insistent, as were the senior management who shared this understanding of Chapel's place, that the building was treated differently from other places in the School, not that it was any more than bricks and mortar, but that what it represented and provided was special and unique. Coming into Chapel was to enter a place where people could be still and reflect, a place where the pupils and staff could distance themselves from the business of the day and could think beyond the material. Chapel was at the beginning of the day and in fact shaped the timetable, particularly on a Friday when lessons were slightly shorter to accommodate a longer Chapel service with a visiting preacher and a fuller liturgy. When prospective parents and visitors asked about the place and importance of the Chapel in the life of the School, I was able to point to the structural priority given to its services and how that was indicative of the priority the School placed upon meeting the spiritual needs of its pupils and staff, even those of faiths other than Christianity and those of no faith.

The world and the School have marched firmly on since the mid-1990s to mid-2000s when I was Chaplain. The challenges have become greater as the pace and direction of change has altered its course. The School is much more of a reflection of the communities and society from which it draws its pupils than ever before, partly because of the digital age and advent of modern communications, but partly because it has to engage more actively in order to prepare its pupils for the uncertainties of the modern world and its advancing challenges. It is no longer possible to be a sort of oasis in leafy greenbelt

Below: Celebrating the 50th anniversary of the Chapel with the Rt Revd Colin James (SH 1940–4), 1988.

Hertfordshire where people can establish a distance from the hustle and bustle of urban life and enjoy education before engaging with the world again. In that sense we have lost something profound. The ability to withdraw and then engage is a good thing; perhaps more than a 'good thing', I would suggest that it is something essential and in short supply in modern society. As human beings we need more than ever to be able to reflect and assess who we are and we are desperate to meet our spiritual needs. Whilst institutionalised religion is in crisis, people do not stop looking to meet this most essential need, but rather look elsewhere and try to find meaning in places where there is none to be found. They end up putting their trust in their treasures which ultimately will be taken away, or rot, or they discover that they are ultimately worthless.

The Revd Daniel Bond (Chaplain from 2007) believes that 'Chapel enables the community to "come and see"': *One of Aldenham's great strengths is its continued and genuine commitment to providing all people with the opportunity to think spiritually and to try and understand the meaning of life. This is the reason why Chapel remains at the centre of this School's life, gifting the community the time and space to reflect, meditate and pray. It is a place where we can honestly face up to the challenges and questions which confront us and actively seek the inner, spiritual strength needed to live the sorts of lives that bring credit to our community, our families and our selves … Chapel enables us all to look back and remember, to grapple with present issues and look hopefully to a future which is informed by the values of the kingdom. Remembrance Day, Visitation Day, OA Day, bidding farewell to our leavers and the celebration of achievements, which ends each of our terms, are all emotive and meaningful events which punctuate Chapel life, providing us all with unforgettable memories of who we are as Aldenham School.*

When Jesus Christ called his first disciples, He told them to 'come and see'. I believe that this is first and foremost the role of the Chapel. Today's lives are lived saturated by global news, multiculturalism, acts of love and acts of hate. Some of these we experience first-hand and others we only witness. Chapel has both the privilege and the serious responsibility to enable the School community to 'come and see' what is going on in the world, both near and far and to enable and equip each individual with the skills to be able to respond to the past and inform the future. Spirituality is all about trying to understand the meaning of life and as the School Chaplain at Aldenham, I hope that all that goes on within the walls of our wonderful Chapel, inspires each person to see the invaluable necessity of nurturing a spiritual journey.

The Rt Revd Hewlett Thompson, former Bishop of Exeter (B 1942–7), reflects on the solid foundation that Aldenham provided: *My own Housemaster's reputation was that of a firm disciplinarian. We were kept busy and one of the many good fruits of this was that there was no bullying. Many Aldenham Masters of that generation were countrymen, with countrymen's sense of respect for nature. Wartime brought then extra burdens. I think we were conscious, then or perhaps later, of how they gave themselves unstintingly to their tasks and without public recognition, which is a sign of Christian ethos. Their aim was for us to be a properly functioning community, an experience essential for satisfactory humanity, and a hallmark of Christianity.*

… For me, Aldenham's ethos of plain living and purposeful activity laid the foundation for my subsequent life because it tackled the question: What is life for? I was grateful to be exposed to the view that education is for service in the world – a better definition, a Christian one, of success, than the view quite widely held today that education's purpose is to lead to jobs that pay well. Aldenham helped me decide on that – and no doubt helped many others – and for me that decision was an essential preliminary to finding that the ultimate truth lies in the person of Jesus Christ.

Above: Tranquility in the Chapel meadow.

Right: A painting of the School community by Ivel Muller in 2007.

chapter five

Living

Although there has been a huge shift from Boarding to Day in recent decades, all pupils are in an important sense still living in community, because that is the nature of the School and one of its greatest strengths. In earlier times the School was fairly isolated. The vast majority of pupils were boarders and spent most of their time within the confines of the School, rarely venturing beyond the local village and only returning home during the School holidays. In recent times the School has become much more open to the wider world. The majority of pupils live within travelling distance of the School and attend on a daily basis. The focal point for their lives is no longer School but home.

This change was not easy to manage for not only were pupils no longer present throughout the School day but there was also an inevitable shift from House- to School-based activities and there was a real risk that community spirit would suffer. In former times Houses were relatively autonomous and Housemasters were totally responsible for the welfare of pupils. Houses seemed to depend for their success on the permanent presence of pupils and on the supervision of all their activities. However, change was achieved without undue trauma and although Houses are now very different places, they can still claim to be very special communities.

HOUSES

The pivotal role of the House in the history of the School has already been covered. But what was it like to live as part of a House community? Two contrasting accounts illustrate how life has changed.

For Basil Maddox (SH 1951–6), 'the first year was rough': *I entered School House Evens at Easter in 1951. The first year was rough, but I was brought up reading Tom Brown's Schooldays, so was expecting much worse. After two weeks to settle in we became 'Boyes'. Tom Brown called them 'Fags' and it was the same thing. We were servants to the senior boys. Modern softness thinks it must have been horrible, but it wasn't. I have no regrets about that time. Those who give orders must first learn to take orders.*

… Every three weeks we had to turn in our cards showing signatures to prove we had worked hard enough as boyes, and we were lined up in the House Library on a Sunday afternoon in front of half-a dozen black-jacketed prefects twice our size who terrified us for an hour or more with questions on our knowledge of the School. Each new boy was issued with a 'Brown Book' and a 'Blue Book', the

School Rules, which you checked off surreptitiously as you broke them. We were examined on all this, and by the end of the year were expected to know the name and House of every boy in the School – 320 of them. This was considered essential – how else could we deliver messages? In the long School photo for 1952 I can still put names to quite a few faces today.

…To ensure our subservience we were required to keep all three buttons of our thick grey tweed jackets done up, which conveniently identified us as boyes. When a prefect wanted a job done, he yelled 'Boye' and the last ones to arrive got the jobs. 'Clean my shoes! Make my bed! Do this washing up! Here's threepence – get me a doughnut from the tuckshop!' Several eager boyes got their cards signed, and my wife blames that custom for all my bad habits to this day! It was a good system as the Sixth Formers had responsibilities they could not fulfil without help, such as carrying 200 folding chairs from the Chapel to the School Hall. As Seating Steward that was one of my jobs in my last year, and I certainly wasn't about to carry them myself.

For Gary Philip (P 1983–8), 'life in Paull's House was pretty straightforward': *You had your appointed place to study; you had your times to complete your work or sport activities; you got spoken down to by the older pupils who were supposed to monitor the homework after supper; you sneakily wrote notes and passed them on to friends when you felt you weren't being watched. Being the 1980s, the hairstyle was pretty important and a majority of pupils sported a 'flock of seagulls' hairstyle, which consisted of an extremely large wedge covering one half of your face. My daughter in the first year of the Prep School had a 'show and tell' and I gave her my 1987 School photo. I do believe that you could see the full face of only half of the School pupils!*

The 1980s saw the start of girls in the Lower and Upper Sixth Forms which was a real head turner for a majority of the boys who were obviously only used to mixing with other boys. In Paull's the girls had separate study areas as well as the obvious dressing and sleeping areas. The study area used to have on one side the 'common area' and the other side the all-weather hockey pitch, so needless to say most of us spent a lot of time in these areas. Having attended an all boys Prep School as well this was a welcome distraction.

first being a list of every boy in the School with his age, House, date of admission and whether his father was an OA (very important). Christian names were not used. The 'Blue Book' was a compendium of the

Left: Kennedy's boys relaxing; Leeman's Games Room; Girls outside the Common Room.

Right: Gilbert House (now McGill's) from a sketch by Leonard Patten.

Below right: A selection of House ties.

The early years at Aldenham were pretty much a blur. The School had an abundance of activities and I was therefore always doing something whether it was sports, Duke of Edinburgh Award, art, House duties or just generally playing with friends. The overriding feeling was that of contentment and fulfilment. Most of us actually enjoyed our School years. This obviously encompassed the fact that most of us got on well and that we made our time special, but I am positive we could not have achieved that sense of enjoyment and fulfilment had we not been in the Aldenham environment. I really do hope my

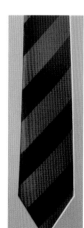

Left: Girls chatting in a study-bedroom in Paull's.

Below: Bedtime in an old-style dormitory.

children experience the same sort of time that *I had and I look forward to hearing their own experiences and stories of the School.*

In his 2010 Visitation Day speech as Head Boy, Jasper Gruenewald (M 2003–10) describes his most enjoyable moments as a boarder: *Great friends, knowledge, support and pastoral care from the teachers. More importantly though, Aldenham seeks to give each individual the best start in their lives and make them all rounded students, unlike other private schools in the local area. Nothing is off limits. Each individual is encouraged to do their best and never settle for anything less.*

My most enjoyable moments at Aldenham occurred when I boarded. There is a great camaraderie between boarders and your friendships with your peers become even closer, not to mention the numerous water fights on Top Field during the summer between the Houses, and the sneaky kebabs and pizzas from the famous Mamuzins during the week. Aldenham has a community spirit I have never encountered before or seen in any other independent school. This is evident in the House system. Every individual feels a part of their House

and they take great pride in their respective Houses, which is clearly apparent during House Competitions. I am proud to say I am a McGillian through and through, although I am sure people from other Houses feel the same way for their own respective House. Today is probably one of the last times the Upper Sixth are all together and may I say it has been a privilege and an honour to have known you all … I wish you all a wonderful time enjoying the excellent gap years and universities you are all going to. Aldenham is a modern and forward thinking School, responsible for some of the happiest of days in my life, so far.

In an article from *The Aldenhamian* entitled 'Scribbles and Nibbles', Richard Jones (Paull's House-master 1972–87) recalls some interesting finds: *The removal of the old lockers and the ventilation shafts in Paull's Lower brought to light a quantity of debris that had been accumulating for all but the full span of its nearly 80 years of existence. Thanks to Mark Jordan's determination for this to be a self-help job, and to his care in preserving what the mice had not destroyed, we now have some glimpses of distant School and family lives …*

… Most fascinating of all are two complete letters, one from a father living at Red House near Winchester, one from a gushing sister at Princess Helena College, Ealing. (I hope that I invade nobody's privacy.)

'Dear old Man' (alas, we never know his name) was being sent 2s 6d to pay for what seems to have been the first 'Wireless Sub'– so presumably the letter dates to the early 1920s; at home father and mother decided they could not afford a radio. 'Daddie' had a firm line on domestic animals: Mrs Day's dog is a 'wretched looking cur' and brother Jack is 'looking forward to scaring the cats with his airgun'.

Beryl Louise writes as if for Daisy Pulls It Off: 'We did have glorious holidays didn't we, pet, as you saw [say?]. Next time we'll aim for the stars and may succeed in hitting the house tops … I've asked Ma to send you the record from Soldiers of the King – "There's something about a soldier". Can you sing that at your concert?' This surely must be from the late 1920s. Beryl Louise was writing to Jimmy and seems to have been a marvellously vivacious and sympathetic sister: 'Only 79 more days of school life left for me.' Again, one reads with some amusement, until the Hardyesque shadows of Time creep up, and the gnawings of the mice make a word difficult to decipher.

Right: Footballers returning from Cooke's Field.

Athletics, archery and basketball are among the many sporting activities available at Aldenham.

SPORT

Sport has always occupied a central place in the life of the School. Austin Galvin (CR 1970 2006) writes: *It has always been felt that, as a small school, Aldenham fights above its weight on the sports front. Sports prowess has been part of the Aldenham ethos, perhaps since 1597.*

...Certainly in the 1970s most afternoons on the timetable were devoted to sport, albeit the major games of football, hockey, cricket and Fives. Academic lessons were in the morning and then squeezed into the late afternoon and early evening slots ... In those days the major sports were controlled with loving

care and professionalism by talented amateurs in the Common Room – Cyril Tyson (football), Donald Newton (hockey), Michael Hetherington (cricket) and Geoffrey Crawshaw (athletics). They were supported by the rest of the Common Room with different abilities with the ethos that, as a schoolmaster, the job implied more than just academic input.

...It was soon obvious that the School was falling behind competitors in hockey and 'minor' sports and activities, and that additional modern facilities were needed. Donald Newton had successfully pushed for a Redgra all-weather hockey pitch and Aldenham was already renowned for the Easter Prep Schools' hockey festival that he organised with the support of Housemasters. But a Sports Hall big enough for indoor hockey? It was particularly important at the time to plan for a wider range of games and activities, particularly with the filling in of the old outdoor swimming pools and the demolition of the squash courts. In due course the Sports Hall arose from the ashes and was there for pupils to diversify their talents and to attract those who would build up a Physical Education Department.

Top: School Mile v. Mill Hill, 1922.

Above: Boxing was popular with earlier generations of boys.

This happened with Sion Thomas (CR 1993–9) persuading the Director of Studies that PE was desirable both as a GCSE and then as an A-level subject. The growth of the PE Department and the continued commitment of the Common Room made it possible for an expansion of what was on offer for the School and the outside community. Bill Waite (Housemaster McGill's 1989–2002) first suggested a Games and Activities programme that was School-based rather than House-based. Kevin Jones (Deputy Head 1997–2004) took this up and a Director of Games and Activities was appointed. This was significant in that sport was now organised on a School basis and the days of a Prae in charge of House exercise were over – as was the House run (or walk)!

Basketball, volleyball, badminton, weights, climbing, pottery, chess, go-karts, drama and dancing were added to the inherited system, plus many more. But inter-school matches are still competitive in all the sports and inter-House competitions are still as important as ever – some things never change.

David Godwin, England International Hockey Player (SH 1971–6) looks back on the foundations of his sporting career and the team play that was so characteristic of Aldenham: *Playing sports at Aldenham has always been about team play. For me, from playing in the Under 14s football team coached by Michael Hetherington to playing for the first team, the emphasis was always on playing as a team and helping each other. As a School with far fewer pupils than many of the other schools we played against, it was just as well we adopted this approach, but it was and is such an important principle.*

I remember some successful football seasons when the first team really excelled and playing alongside individuals such as John Baugh, Andy Clare and Kofi Appenteng. A great deal of talent and some great characters were all held together by Cyril Tyson, who instilled the basics in all of us and taught us the benefits of hard work. This included the drills and practice sessions that you needed to perfect to ensure that you were able to perform on the big stage when it really mattered.

The same principles applied in hockey, where we were fortunate to have Donald Newton as our coach and mentor. We did not always have the best talent, but we played to the best of our ability and were always hard to beat. I remember us beating Kingston Grammar School 1–0 at the Oxford Festival, and they were probably the best school team in the country at the time with internationals sitting on the bench. Their coach was not impressed but I know Donald enjoyed the win.

I was fortunate enough to play football for England Public Schools, and also play hockey for England at full international level. What I do clearly remember is competing and playing against players who were much more skilled than me, but who didn't have the determination and fight when it really mattered. It was an important lesson and the grounding I received at Aldenham, the desire never to give up, stood me in good stead.

Playing as a team is not just about sports. It gives you a foundation that you can use in all parts of your life and help you, and those around you, become the best that you can be. Even now as a banker I frequently use the analogy of a football team to help my staff understand the benefits of working together. I will always be grateful to Aldenham for teaching me that important lesson.

Richard Hall (K 1969–74) recalls the 'heyday of OA football': *The 1970s were a great period for football at the School and for the OAs, who were supported by Cyril Tyson, the Master in charge of football at School at the time. He was able to nurture the growing crop of talent – the pinnacle was playing against the Arsenal youth team at the end of the season. The early 1970s saw some great quality footballers, the Appenteng Brothers, Andy Clare and John Baugh who all went on to play for the English Public Schools. Cyril used to arrange a pre-season tour playing in Lancashire against the top grammar schools of Bury, Bolton and Blackburn – this started to give Aldenham an edge over our local schools. The School side was significantly stronger than the OAs during this period and I was lucky enough to Captain the strongest ever Aldenham football side when we lost only one game in the season, an away match, 1–0 to Brentwood (the only time I cried at School – when the final whistle went). But revenge was to be so sweet a few years later.*

OAFC success began through Steve Hitchens (OAFC Captain) who worked hard at recruiting the best footballers (I played while still at School at the age of 16) and he kept together the nucleus of the best players at the time. The most important catalyst was when Phil Smith returned from Canada to teach at Aldenham – he became the pivot around which the team developed. The 1976 team began to understand how to play to our strengths, work hard as a team and keep it simple. Yet the belief that we could be winners was through beating better 'footballing' sides (Brentwood, Cholmeleians, Chigwell and Lancing) and the 1976–7 Team won the Arthurian League

title against this seriously talented opposition. Sweet revenge was just around the corner in 1979 when we beat Old Brentwoodians at Crystal Palace 1–0 in the Arthur Dunn final. It was a day to remember – especially the minibus return journey back to the Three Horsehoes to continue the celebrations. The 77/78 Team had real class…

In addition to football, hockey and cricket many other sporting activities flourished at Aldenham. None more so than Eton Fives, a sport in which the School gained a considerable reputation. Graham Pulsford (M 1971–5) recalls an inspirational coach: *I enjoyed all the sports at School and especially the game of Eton Fives. It is truly a game of hazards. You can't play Fives without learning to accept outrageous twists of luck, with the best of plans being frustrated by the ball taking an unexpected bounce after hitting a ledge or angle. I had the pleasure of being taught by David Barker (B 1953–9, CR 1969–*

Above left: Under 15As match versus Highgate in 2007.

Above: The OAs team that won the Arthur Dunn Cup final against Old Brentwoodians in 1979.

Left: Final of the Arthur Dunn Cup, Old Aldenhamians v. Old Brightonians, 1913.

Far right: An energetic game of Eton Fives c.1930 (above) and (below) DR Barker (B 1953–9) and U Mohammad (P 1953–9), winners of the Public Schools Fives Competition in 1959.

John Dewes (B 1940–5)

On Wednesday 7 July 2010, former England Test Cricketer and Old Boy of Aldenham School John Dewes was the special guest at the inaugural cricket match of a Select XI against Aldenham's 1st XI side. John Dewes attended Aldenham School 1940–5 and was Captain of the XI in his last year at the School. He went on to represent Cambridge University and Middlesex CCC before playing five tests for England between 1948–51.

...The game was played in the right spirit with the John Dewes XI batting first. They scored a challenging 236 for 8 before declaring half an hour after lunch. Rishi Batra, a promising Year 11 leg spinner, bowled beautifully, recording his best figures of the season 3-19. The pick of the batsmen was Tom Pettet (ex-Aldenham School 1st XI Captain) who scored 80 before being bowled just before the interval. John Emburey did get to the crease but was left 0* when the declaration came!

In reply the 1st XI lost an early wicket and then really struggled against the spin of Simon Weale (ex-Oxford University) and John Emburey. They were finally bowled out for 129 which meant the John Dewes XI won the match by 110 runs. Wills Collier managed a classy 25 runs including five boundaries, whilst the shot of the day came from Max Raby, who deposited a ball from John Emburey into the next field beyond the School – a huge 6 and a moment I am sure he will remember for a long time to come!

At the tea interval the Headmaster, Mr James Fowler, presented Mr Dewes with a framed England Jumper that John Dewes had worn in his first Test. A tree was also planted to commemorate the inaugural match. It was a very special occasion and with over 50 Old Aldenhamians attending, it will now be added to the calendar as the last game of the season for the Aldenham 1st XI.

Press Release
July 2010

79), who was an understated but brilliant player winning the Public Schools competition twice. For practice he would get us to stand just outside the back right of the court and throw the ball onto the front wall and then 'dead' into the box. When we had accomplished this, he would get us to throw with our weaker arm. David would consistently score 3 or 4 out of 5 with either arm and none of us could get close!

ACTIVITIES

Aldenham's distinctive approach to the extra-curricular aspects of School life goes well beyond the games field and includes a whole range of activities that have developed over the years. Sometimes they grew up as an integral part of the Aldenham experience – Community Service, Combined Cadet Force, Duke of Edinburgh Award Scheme and International Expeditions. Often they were inspired by particular individuals.

Over the years, a large number of activities took place, catering for a wide range of disparate interests. In the pages of *The Aldenhamian* there are reports from nearly 30 different clubs and societies that have met over the last few decades. Many waxed and waned according to the enthusiasms of individual pupils and staff, but others were a feature of school life for most of this time. Some societies were extensions of academic subjects – Science, Geography, Languages, History and English, or were closely associated with the wider cultural life of the School – Music, Drama, Art, Debating and Public Speaking, and *Les Philosophes*, a Sixth Form society which invited speakers and held regular debates on a range of intellectual and contemporary problems. Other groups met to pursue particular hobbies – Modelling, Bridge, Chess, Stamps, Photography, Archaeology and Amateur Radio. A few pupils were involved with

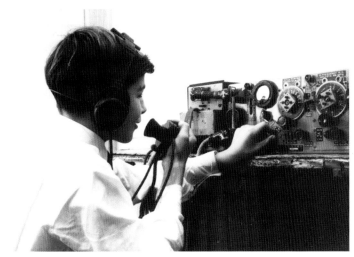

particular projects – the Aldenham School Press, the School Meteorological Station, *The Aldenhamian, Platt's Chronicle*. The forerunners of Information & Communication Technology (ICT) and Design Technology (DT) were also popular activities.

The Aldenham School Press was an important part of the Aldenham scene for many years, as is recalled by Mark Jordan (P 1981–6), one of its most active members: *In the days long before desktop publishing, laser printers and, of course, Health and Safety, the Aldenham School Press (ASP) produced most of the School's internal printing as well as undertaking small-scale commercial printing for pupils, parents, local businesses and residents.*

Above: Esmond Burrows (SH 1971–7) prepares a machine for printing.

Centre: The Radio Club was an early activity with enthusiastic members.

Left: Weather readings are still taken daily and sent to the Metereological Office.

Operating as a mixture of a society and a business and run by the pupils during term time, the ASP produced many hundreds of different items from Visitation Day invitations through to play programmes and the weekly Exeat chits.

Located on the ground floor of the Arts and Technical Block, the printing room contained letterpress printing equipment, including around 100 cases (drawers) of lead type, and presses ranging in size from a hand-operated Adana to a fully automatic Heidelberg Platen. The process, painstaking by modern standards, involved each lead letter being taken from a case and assembled into a frame, which was locked into the press to be inked and pressed onto the paper. Once the printing was finished the type was distributed back to its correct compartment.

The Press also boasted a large electric guillotine, a mechanical stitching machine, a lithographic printing press (mainly used for photographs), a dark room for plate development and a 'new' technology at the time, phototypesetting. Thus the well-equipped ASP funded its own activities and even showed a profit some terms!

The ASP closed down during the mid-1990s as modern computer technology replaced the traditional letterpress printing methods.

THE COMBINED CADET FORCE (CCF)

The CCF has had a long history in the School as has already been documented. Chris Arkell (B 1946–51, CR 1962–93) describes his time with the CCF in two very different roles: *There are two periods during which I was closely involved in the CCF: the first between 1947 and 1952, on the receiving end, as it were, and the second, between 1962 and 1972 as a member of the directing staff.*

During the first period we were all aware of the fact that we would have to do National Service when we left Aldenham. This fact meant that those Friday afternoons were important for us to get to grips with rifles and the cleaning of them, belts and gaiters and the blancoing and polishing of them. Inspection and Drill then followed, carried out by Hugh Kirkwood, Geoffrey Crawshaw, Raymond Griggs and Chief Petty Officer Williams in the RN section and of course the dreaded figure of Sergeant-Major Buckingham, our much respected PT teacher who wielded absolute power over his troops. We also learned basic tactics, drill, map reading and how to fire (in my case largely

Above: The OTC parading on the School field soon after it was formed in 1908.

Left: Cadets taking part in a Home Guard exercise in 1944.

Below: Air Cadet Training in the 1940s.

inaccurately) .22 rifles. The Grand Old Duke of York would have been proud of us as we marched with the School Bugle and Drum Band to Aldenham Church on Remembrance Sunday.

The second period of my involvement with the CCF was quite different. I could give orders, (largely disregarded), and gaze with bemusement at the troops assembled … The highlight of the period was the inspired leadership of Ken Barnard in Arduous Training, an absolutely excellent scheme sponsored by the Army to teach the troops self-reliance, confidence and resilience on expeditions in some of the wildest and most testing parts of the UK. Snowdonia, the

Right: CCF Biennial Inspection, 2009.

Cairngorms, Dartmoor, the Brecon Beacons, and even the Mourne mountains became our training grounds, a far cry from Letchmore Heath! Many colleagues joined us: Geoffrey Crawshaw, Ernie Wheeler, Michael Palmer, Arthur Hearnden and as a civilian adviser, Michael Hetherington on our wonderful expeditions along Crib Goch, navigating across Dartmoor and dealing with cold, snowy or wet conditions in the Cairngorms…

Three things emerge from all this: they are the ability to accept discipline and inspection and probably more important, the development of confidence and leadership in arduous conditions and not least, the joy of friendship and comradeship.

Although the CCF was still generously supported by the Armed Forces, it became increasingly difficult to find officers and in 1989 it closed. However, in 2006 it was revived, as Molly Barton, Development Manager, explains: *As a former officer in the Women's Royal Naval Service I was invited to join the Combined Cadet Force (CCF) when it was relaunched in 2006 after a break of 17 years. We were fortunate to be able to take advantage of the skills of Alan Cockerill, Paul Stanbury and Tom Kupfer, who had plenty of CCF experience in previous schools and WO1 Fritzy Albrecht, joined us as our Senior Staff Instructor (SSI)*

to keep us on our toes. The new cadets grappled with polishing boots – shoe polish being unknown to the modern pupil – and wearing the correct kit for the weekly parade. When Martineau's relocated to Kennedy's, the CCF was given its own space in the Near and Far Block to create an HQ, using the playground behind as a parade ground.

In December 2008 Queens' School, Bushey joined our CCF and we became one of the first six schools in the London Area to form a partnership CCF with a school from the maintained sector. Cadets from both schools parade every Thursday afternoon and take part in a varied training programme and activities, ranging from drill and weapons training to flying, to the newly formed drum corps and adventurous training in Wales. HMS Albion's connection with the Brewers' Company has meant many cadets have had the opportunity to go to sea even though we don't have a naval section. The first biennial inspection, in October 2009, was carried out with pride by former pupil, Field Marshal Lord Vincent of Coleshill GBE KCB DSO, who also arranged for the Golding Sword to be presented to the CCF by the military tailor and parent of a former pupil, Mr GD Golding. The sword is presented annually to the best Aldenham Cadet.

The CCF represents the School in the wider community, particularly in the annual Remembrance Service on the Village Green in Letchmore Heath, and the skills of discipline, leadership and comradeship are taught and remain as valid now as when the CCF originally formed.

THE DUKE OF EDINBURGH
AWARD SCHEME

The Duke of Edinburgh Award Scheme has been running at Aldenham for many years and some of its most distinctive features have been the expeditions mounted by David MacGregor (CR 1982–99) and others: *Being a firm believer in self-reliance and ambition, I made it my job, when running the expeditionary side of the Award Scheme between 1982 and the mid-1990s, to take boys and girls to the most demanding parts of the UK.*

After the first outing to the Brecon Beacons, then, from early days, ploughing through the muddy 'groughs' in the Edale district of Derbyshire, to clinging onto the narrow ridges of Crib Goch in Snowdonia, then to the steep sides of the Lakes and so to Scotland, particularly the Cairngorms and Kintail, where we tackled the toughest hills in the country, I put pupils through as demanding a set of expeditions as any school in the country. Highlights were the all-night midsummer walk through Glen Lichd (Kintail) in search of missing girls who weren't missing; managing a group of 22 in the Cairngorms by myself before Health and Safety had been invented; Toby Boon's disappearance and subsequent recovery from a peat bog; scaling all seven Munros of the South Cluanie Ridge in one day; the wettest day of my life on Snowdon and a wild camp in remote Ardgour.

I was fortunate in my colleagues. Richard Jones, the most resolute and imperturbable driver I have ever met, drove to such unusual locations as Kinloch Hourn, the eastern base of Mam Soul (Loch Monar) and some unusual spots on Skye. One could not ask for a better person to be with. The late Ken Barnard was often on hand to offer his genial help, and the late Michael Hetherington – who managed to compleat (sic) his Munros on his 70th birthday, before his tragic disappearance in the Drakensberg – often came along with his happy nature, tremendous fitness and (sometimes) cakes. With the possible exception of J Archer Thompson, James Howel, the finest climber which Aldenham has produced, came back on several occasions and was an immense help…

I think about 1,500 pupils probably went on expeditions during my time at Aldenham. About 90 per cent of them self-evidently really enjoyed themselves. And I firmly believe that, through participating, they all grew in maturity and self-awareness.

At the end of 2010 the Duke of Edinburgh Award Scheme continues to flourish at Aldenham, with 35 pupils currently following the programme. The Bronze Award was recently awarded to 12 pupils, while five others completed their Silver and 18 are working towards their Gold. Expeditions for Bronze are operated in Hertfordshire and for Silver and Gold in the Peak District and Dorset.

But expeditions went well beyond the Duke of Edinburgh Award Scheme and under David MacGregor's leadership the School mounted some impressive international expeditions, to the Chinese Pamirs (1989), Zanskar Himalaya (1992) and the Dzhungarian Alatau, Kazakhstan (1998): *These expeditions were an extension of my Duke of Edinburgh's Award belief in expeditions as a way of generating self-awareness and personal maturity. What they had in common were talented youngsters and an interest in unexplored areas and unclimbed peaks. We made, on these three expeditions, no fewer than 16 first ascents, on heights ranging from 3,300 metres to 5,500 metres above sea level.*

The Pamirs expedition was inspired by Sir Chris Bonington's Mt Kongur expedition to south-west China. Sir Chris went on to be Patron of four of my Central Asian expeditions. We were helped enormously by Sally Westmacott, who taught music at Aldenham in the 1980s, and her husband, Mike, the second-youngest member of the 1953 Everest

Mark Hancock (CR 1994–2002) on the Dzhungarian Alatau Expedition, Kazakhstan, 1998.

Right: Zanskar, 1992.

Right: Zanskar, 1992.

expedition; their combined talents and advice were invaluable. Only six months after the Tiananmen Square massacre, with China in dreadful ferment, we travelled over the newly opened but still terrifying Karakoram Highway, at the time the highest surfaced road in the world, from Rawalpindi (Pakistan) to Kashgar. The Pamirs resemble giant Cairngorms; good snow-climbing techniques were essential. We climbed three peaks, over 5,400 metres high and carried out some dramatic exploration. I subsequently had an article published in the Alpine Journal *(1991), the most prestigious mountaineering publication anywhere. The boys who took part I recall as a vintage crew: James Howel, David Kilborn, John Turner and Owen Williams in particular.*

Following Mike Westmacott's advice, we then turned our attention to Zanskar, which lies in 'Little Tibet', northern India. The ground was rockier and crumblier than in the Pamirs, so perhaps less satisfying, but the scenery was more classically beautiful. Two difficulties occurred: the climbing leader and two boys had an accident when a belay failed on a summit ridge. All three fell 244 metres, fortunately on snow. Nick (the climbing leader), had to return home with a dislocated shoulder, but the boys, Robert May and Owen Williams, survived with

cuts and bruises, the only 'serious' accident on any of my expeditions. And on leaving the mountains, we just avoided a terrorist attack which burnt down a nearby town. Evacuation under military escort by moonlight was a hair-raising experience in the utterly beautiful land of Kashmir.

The third adventure combined with Marlborough College and Shrewsbury School for the first European expedition to the newly opened post-Soviet area of north-east Kazakhstan, to an unheard-of range, but which is as long and high as the Alps. Despite appalling boulder fields, dangerous river-crossings (where I almost lost my life) and hopeless maps we enjoyed a riot of first ascents, all around the 4,000-metre mark (including CJ Meadows's heroic first, a week after catching bronchitis). This expedition ended with a party on the shores of Lake Kapchegai, an apparently scenic spot wrecked by Soviet ecological unfriendliness.

The participating boys were formidably strong, skilful, team-spirited and friendly. My colleagues were brilliant; parents were immensely supportive; the Brewers were more than generous. These were, in School terms, high achievements: memorable, life-changing and enjoyable.

chapter six

Learning

Learning takes place throughout a school career and the measure of a good school is the extent to which it provides a stimulating learning environment. Aldenham is such a place with its formal academic curriculum and teaching from highly qualified staff. It is also a place where pupils are not only schooled but educated, and where they not only acquire skills but also engage with culture. It is a place where they receive vocational and careers guidance of a high order and where they receive support and guidance in the process of university applications and have the opportunity to undertake supervised work experience. Aldenham is also a place where they learn from each other in a wide range of activities within what might be broadly described as the informal curriculum.

The academic curriculum is the formal framework for learning in the School but 'is subject to a variety of pressures' as David Watts (Director of Studies from 2002) explains: *Within the School community the pressures come from teachers, parents and pupils. Teachers will want to have the time to teach a particular course in a particular way. Parents will want their children to be successful and taught the way that they were taught, both in style and content. Pupils will have aspirations that need to be educated, directed and satisfied. Often quite ephemeral factors will create a pressure. For example, a change in style or staffing may lead to a perceived success amongst the students and a greater take up in the subject. Similarly the family holiday destination has created a greater pressure for Spanish than French.*

External bodies have also had an impact on the curriculum. Government legislation has been more intrusive than ever. The national curriculum has necessitated adjustments to the curriculum at Aldenham, but the focus on results is both unhealthy and unhelpful. Examining bodies vie with one another to create the subject specification for a generation of school children. GCSE and A level compete with a variety of qualifications, many claiming to be the new gold standard but often simply more elitist. Never has the independence of Aldenham been more precious than now in responding to these pressures.

Over the past 20 years subjects have come and gone, often reflecting national trends in popularity. Politics and Social Biology have slipped quietly out of the curriculum; Economics and Ancient History disappeared for a while only to enjoy a resurgence

in popularity of late in slightly different forms. Other subjects have been added, Media Studies at A level, Dance at GCSE and Drama and Textiles at both. French has ceased to be compulsory (although a foreign language to GCSE still is).

In recent times the School changed from a six-day week to a five-day week and at the same time changed the length of lessons. This meant fewer, longer lessons per week. The challenge or opportunity was to rethink the shape of the curriculum. The core and compulsory elements were quickly identified and then the philosophy for choosing the options worked out. Into the core went Religious Studies, which provides an ethical and philosophical framework for all the knowledge acquired in School. Next Mathematics, English, the Sciences, a Foreign Language and IT were in. This then left a number of subjects from the humanities (History, Geography, Classical Civilisation), creative subjects (Art, Design Technology) and performance-based subjects (Dance, Drama, Music, PE) which needed to be represented but would be an option in later years. Given such an upheaval there were necessarily losers at various stages. Some of this could be alleviated by giving a more generous allocation at a different level of the School. Some could not and this has left us having to work that little bit harder in the time that we have with the students.

Curriculum time aside, three main factors have had a big impact on what goes on in the classroom.

Right: A Chemistry demonstration by Tom Kupfer (CR 2007–).

Below: A Chemisty Laboratory in the 1950s.

Far right: A Biology class.

There is now a greater understanding of how students learn, what sort of learners they are and how they can be more actively involved. Twenty years ago a kinaesthetic learner – someone who learns by doing rather than hearing or seeing – was liable to have a difficult time in the classroom. Now there is an expectation that in the best-planned lessons the 'doers' are involved and are learning just as much as the 'seers' and 'hearers'. There is also a greater understanding of the barriers to learning and how these may be managed in children. Two decades ago dyslexia was a rarely mentioned condition, but now its impact on a significant number of students is recognised and accommodated. Finally, 20 years ago a classroom looked pretty much the same wherever you were: a board to write on and pens or chalks to write on it were the tools of the trade of all teachers – as indeed they had been for the last 100 years. Now the board is sidelined by projectors, interactive whiteboards and other technology. Lessons do not end in the classroom but through the web can be brought in to the home or the study in the House.

Looking to the future, the only thing one can be certain of is that change will continue and be just as unpredictable. Twenty years ago there were just two computers in the Science Department. As a teacher *at that time I would never have envisaged sending revision notes to students' iPhones!*

Terry Ford (CR from 1979) argues that one of the most significant pressures on Aldenham, as on other schools, has been the demand for accountability and the attempt to measure success using league tables: *Aldenham, like all schools, faces tensions between the demands of lessons and the desire to provide a wide range of extra-curricular activities, but, because of its structure as a boarding school and its history and membership of the Headmasters' and Headmistresses' Conference, these tensions are greater than average. Added to this, in recent years there has been a marked drive to measure and to assess the value of establishments and their activities, and to hold individuals within those establishments to account for the degree of success achieved. This has manifested itself in the form of targets and league tables. These need quantifiable outcomes that can be easily and (apparently) accurately measured. For schools the metric has been largely exam results as they are easy to quantify and the figures that are derived appear valid to compare.*

Unfortunately, league tables are a potentially misleading measure, especially for a school like Aldenham, which is not highly selective in terms of academic ability. Schools with this approach will inevitably appear lower down than equally good schools with a selective entry. Only when the tables could be constructed on a more sophisticated basis to show 'value added', i.e. whether a school had managed to help its pupils to achieve better results than would have been expected given their ability and position

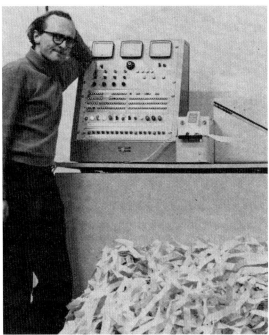

Above: Boys processing information with punched paper tape in the early days of computing at Aldenham.

Left: The School's first computer arrived in 1974 on a lorry and was made operationalby CH Moller (CR 1974–7).

Below left: Paul Spencer (CR 1985–) with pupils.

on entering the school, could the tables hope to give an accurate reflection of the quality of a school. Even then, methodological problems remain, for, perhaps perversely, if such a table were to be produced, a school with a highly selective admissions process would not show up as a high 'value added' establishment as there would be no scope for its pupils to perform better than expected. As a consequence, over the last decade, schools like Aldenham with a very low hurdle for entry have, along with other schools which have very high hurdles for admission, withdrawn from the league tables and sought to demonstrate their quality and value through other methods…

TECHNOLOGY

The School's first computer was delivered, quite literally, on the back of a lorry, in the early 1970s. It was an Elliot 920 machine and it filled a small room. It was donated to the School by the Elliot company. Although engineers from the company did all they could to get the machine running, it really awaited the arrival of someone within the School who had the necessary skills and commitment. In 1974, Chris Moller was appointed to teach Physics and had the expertise and enthusiasm to tackle the job. In due course, other machines were donated or purchased, and computing became a thriving activity. Eventually, the Elliot machine was replaced by an Apple computer, and that in turn by a number of BBC machines when a new Computer Department was created under David Mead in 1982. With the advent of these facilities, the emphasis soon shifted from programming to applications and the modern era of computing began. The subject flourished and expanded both within and outside the curriculum. In due course, a modern generation of PCs was purchased and, by the mid-1990s, networking of the School began. The rest, as they say, is history.

It also became increasingly clear in the 1970s that the provision of other aspects of technical education within the School was inadequate and lagged behind other similar schools. The opening of the new Arts and Technical Block provided the space to begin to expand these facilities, but little thought had been given to how these facilities might develop. Part

115

establish these activities with adequate facilities and specialist teaching. In the late 1980s the old Chapel was converted to a workshop and money was spent on tools and equipment. The subject was introduced into the curriculum.

However, it soon became clear that something was missing. If Aldenham was aiming to teach technology, then it had to be approached from a different direction. Technology needed to be seen as a problem-solving activity in which at least as much weight was placed on the design of the solution as on its realisation. To date, too much attention had been focused on the realisation and too little on the design. This had to change. To achieve this, Alun Pickford was appointed; he had been specifically trained to teach technology, and had the necessary graphic design skills as well as skills of the more traditional craft teacher. In the early 1990s, the workspace was redesigned and re-equipped and the subject relaunched. It quickly became established with very successful GCSE and A level groups and became an important 'centre of excellence' within the School.

of the problem arose from the emphasis that had been traditionally placed in technical education on the practical aspects of the subject – woodwork and metalwork. It was felt that the first step in developing technical subjects within the curriculum was to re-

DRAMA

As one of a number of distinguished producers of plays at Aldenham, Richard Jones (CR 1962–94) summarises the achievements of both pupils and staff in a wide range of dramatic productions over the years: *From the proud opening of the Assembly Hall and its stage in the 1950s to the construction of the enviable new theatre facilities, there was a struggle with the corset of the very 1950s proscenium arch and the minute wings' space. The desirable aim of involving as many Aldenhamians as possible in any staged drama was too often restricted. Nevertheless, over the years, apart from the obvious actors in School and senior and junior House performances, there were directors, script adapters, stage designers and set builders, electricians, costumiers ... all gaining a sense of being in a more varied creative team than could be experienced on any playing field.*

Some productions burst out off the stage to utilise the body of the Hall, notably several of David MacGregor's. In Marlowe's Doctor Faustus, the mouth of Hell emitted smoke and fire from under the gallery; for several Shakespearian plays we sat around the centre of the Hall or even on the stage to watch Hamlet die, or Beatrice and Benedick dance their requited love across a painted map of the world. For the second part of Brecht's The Good Woman of Setzuan we had to move to the uncomfortable benches of the Dining Hall. The Chapel, with its open spaces, was also sometimes used. Musicals such as The Girl Next Door, and opera such as Dido and Aeneas, with Alan Vening's help also widened horizons, as, in other ways, did visits by professional groups from the Watford Palace Theatre.

In the early 1970s an outdoor stage was constructed with the help of pupils. Further back, in August 1964 and 1965, the 'school plays' A Man for All Seasons and The Taming of the Shrew were taken to Cornwall for performance in the Minack Theatre. Here was a breakthrough for Aldenham, as there were girls in the casts, and here Bruce Alexander – later a member of the Royal Shakespeare Company (and A Touch of Frost!) – began his public acting career. Aldenham groups saw him several times among the regular and varied theatre outings around the country.

But it was not only the pupils who performed. Arthur Hearnden (CR 1959–67) recalls a number of staff productions in the 1960s: *In a gallant attempt to help the Sixties to swing in Aldenham, the Common*

Room put on a series of plays in the School Hall. A number of conditions attached to this new venture. Tickets would be sold to parents whose sons could be with them in the audience. All proceeds would go to support the Aldenham Boys' Club in Kentish Town. The plays would be of no conceivable literary merit. And no photos would be taken in order to ensure that there would be nothing for posterity to remember them by.

Now, 50 years on, posterity is fighting back with these erratic recollections, for which the sole accurate basis is the title of each play and the year in which it was performed. With the 'man (and woman) of the match' approach to sporting entertainment in mind, a few performances do vaguely stick in the memory:

Who Goes There (1960) saw Michael Palmer as guardsman Arthur Crisp leaping to attention every time he was caught in a compromising situation while in pursuit of his voluptuous quarry, Margaret Davis as Christina Deed.

Top: David Brewerton (McGill's 1957–62) in The Imaginary Invalid *by Moliere, December 1961.*

Above: The Clandestine Marriage *by David Garrick and George Colman, 1959.*

Right: Tom Wainwright (McGill's 2004–11) and Margaux Stones (P 2009–11) taking the leads in Macbeth, *2010.*

Doctor in the House (1961) had David Robertson as the famous surgeon, Sir Lancelot Spratt, struggling to enunciate 'subcutaneous fat' under the eagle eye of battleship Matron, Joy Roseveare.

All For Mary (1962) featured Tony Thornhill-Cole as Victor Monteny, the lascivious rake eyeing up his friend's wife as a likely conquest, but held at bay by the formidable Nanny Cartwright, played by Pat Stagg.

Simon and Laura (1963) saw Chris Arkell as Simon Foster and Vera Wallace-Hadrill as Laura, his wife, in a theatrically trendy household, outscoring one another in vituperously witty repartee.

Farewell, Farewell, Eugene (1965) featured Michael Benson, a guest actor brought in from Radlett to play Mick Delaney, the Irish waster and foil for scattily genteel widow Minerva Goody, played by Helen Wright.

The programmes record that over the six years exactly 40 members of the Common Room or their families appeared on stage, having given up many evenings to rehearsals. The productions were made possible by the benign tolerance of successive Headmasters and an industrious backstage team led first by Michael Hetherington and then Donald Newton. They marshalled an army of stagehands, electricians, property mistresses, make-up artists, printers, and musical effects experts who put the audience in the right mood before curtain-up with blaring recordings of Herb Alpert and his Tijuana Brass.

There were one or two further productions in the 1970s, most notably *The Dutch Uncle* produced by Peter Gough in 1974. It was first presented as a leaving entertainment at Cambridge in 1956, and its adaptation by Alan Vening, who wrote the music, and Peter Gough who produced the Aldenham version, provided perfect end-of-term entertainment.

Many pupils were inspired by their experience of the creative arts at Aldenham, including Jonathan Brett (M 1963–8), now a Hollywood film producer, who remembers Orson Welles and Oliver Reed visiting the School: *I spent a very happy five years at Aldenham between 1963 and 1968 as a member of McGill's House … While not an over-achiever on the playing field (!), I made up for it with my interest in the arts, which were very well supported during my time there. I believe I acted in virtually every School play and House play, and due to the proximity of the film studios at Elstree and Borehamwood, I was able to see moviemaking at first hand at the School. I have an indelible memory of watching Orson Welles and Oliver Reed seated in a stationary open-top sports car, parked on the cricket pitch next to Paull's, surrounded by a large movie crew, directed by Michael Winner, in I'll Never Forget What's'isname.*

I have to believe that this memory, combined with my interest in theatre at Aldenham (under the auspices of Richard Jones and Arthur Hearnden), helped guide me to where I have ended up today,

Above left: Supporting a production from the Apthorp Technical Suite.

Above: Characters from a production of Orwell's Animal Farm *in 2009.*

based in New York, where I have spent the past 20 years as a motion picture screenwriter and producer. My films include *She Devil* (starring Meryl Streep), which I produced; *Turbulence* (starring Ray Liotta), which I wrote; the Oscar-nominated *Dutch Master* (starring Mira Sorvino), which I wrote and produced; and the forthcoming *Occupant*, which I wrote and produced and which is due for release in early 2011.

I enjoyed my time at Aldenham greatly and think back to my time there, and my memories, with great affection.

The conversion of the Assembly Hall into the new School Theatre in 2007 coincided with renewed interest in Drama. It became a GCSE and A level subject and the range of productions increased dramatically. The quality of the productions and the enthusiasm of those taking part inspired the editor of *The Good Schools Guide* to write, 'Someone here cares about real theatre and gets on with it, inspiring others along the way'. An account in *The Aldenhamian* of 2009 gives a flavour of one year's activity: *beginning with the Senior Show, One Flew Over the Cuckoo's Nest, in November 2008. An amazing feat of ensemble acting, with David Cotter sparkling in the role of McMurphy and Verity Gosden utterly convincing as Nurse Ratchett. Every single member of the cast gave a superb performance, with long-serving staff commenting that it was the best show they had ever seen at Aldenham.*

In December, the A-level Drama students presented their own devised shows, while January saw new Drama teacher Sam Sugarman's Middle School production of Sparkleshark, a tale of imaginative youngsters creating stories on a rooftop. This was a very capable ensemble production featuring a promising array of young actors. In March, the GCSE productions God (a play), Accidental Death of an Anarchist, Bouncers, Speed the Plow, The Wind in the Willows, Trafford Tanzi and The Nun's Priest's Tale produced a crop of great results for the performers. The A level shows were an engaging night out: The Taming and Rhinocerisation featured Year 13 adaptations whilst Year 12 gave us individual monologues followed by The Maids and The Caretaker.

The Senior House Drama Competition followed the theme of Superheroes and every House rose to the occasion with productions of Batman, Spiderman, Wolverine, Superman, The Hulk and Dr Doom. Martineau's House Drama in May took Shakespearean plays as its theme and it was a delight to see so many talented

Right: Kennedy's Unison Song.

performers coming up through the School. More was seen of Martineau's abundance of talent in the Junior Production of Revolting Rhymes, most ably directed by Philip Wright, new Head of History. The final theatre offerings of the year were from Year 10 with their devised plays The Lighthouse's Tale and Flawle$s.

The incredible members of the Aldenham School Stage Crew, led by Andrew Stead with support from James Glanville, Paul Spencer and Julie Bannister, were staunchly there for every production.

MUSIC

Geoffrey Barker (CR 1965–99) had a long career teaching music at Aldenham and in a survey, which he calls 'a semiquaver's view', he indentifies some of the highlights: *My introduction to music at Aldenham was being invited to play in the orchestra for a performance of Messiah in March 1965, shortly before joining the staff in September of that year. I was quite unprepared for the style and atmosphere of the occasion, presided over by Bill Hook, the Director of Music. The Chapel was full to overflowing: the School, staff, parents and special guests, not to mention the performers squeezed into every available space. The whole School took part – I had never heard the 'Hallelujah' chorus given such treatment and I soon learned that this was how things were done at Aldenham. Everyone who could – and some who thought they could not – participated. The effect was stunning.*

The musical calendar consisted of a series of termly events – House Music Competition, Carol Service, Oratorio (later Spring) Concert, and Visitation Day

service in which the whole School was involved, and the Beck Competition for soloists. During my first term, I was approached by a number of senior pupils asking if I would organise some less formal concerts where solo and small ensemble items could be included. Thus was born the Music at Five series held on half-days during the week. The music staff responded to the challenge and presented a complementary series of evening concerts on Saturdays. A regular performer at these concerts was Jack Waddell, a wonderful colleague and friend, who lent his considerable talents as oboist and singer to the musical life of the School. A regular feature of summer terms was his Serenade Concert performed on the veranda of the Pavilion while the audience relaxed on the grass, some pretending to revise for A and O level exams! …

When Alan Vening became Director in 1973, whole-school music was given an enormous boost by

having a great many compositions specially written, not only for big occasions, but also for the daily services. No doubt some of these were partly inspired by the new pipe organ, christened magnificently at a concert in 1977. These special compositions built up into a remarkable library that rightly reflects the inclusiveness of Aldenham's musical tradition. When the Music Masters' Conference came to Aldenham in May 1982, Alan composed an entire cantata – Behold the Music Master – with text by Peter Vincent, for the occasion, and had this to say about it in The Aldenhamian of October 1982: 'The "philosophy" of the Conference was to involve as many people as possible, i.e. the whole School, Edge Grove, St Margaret's Bushey and Beechwood Park (schools that Aldenham regularly collaborated with). The tradition of whole-school unison singing was handed to me by my predecessor (WGH) at a time when virtually every other school in the country had abandoned it. This is what we were able to offer the Music Masters' Association and the School responded marvellously well.' Believe me, there is nothing more inspiring than hearing the whole School in full voice!

There were always opportunities to perform, but the School was fortunate in the provision of individual instrumental lessons, delivered by a loyal, imaginative and experienced team of peripatetic teachers. This enabled us to maintain an excellent School Orchestra, plus wind and brass groups as well as fostering the more soloistic element. During most

Above left: Wind Quintet with Bill Hook (Director of Music 1948-73) in 1963.

Above: Recording in the Music Technology Suite.

Left: Making music in the Waddell Recital Room in 2000.

Right: April Koyejo (P 2008–10) singing in the House Music Competition, 2009.

of my time at Aldenham, nearly a third of the School took instrumental music lessons and with the opening of Martineau's House in 1993, this total rose.

When Alan Vening retired in 1994, John Wyatt joined me, and we ran the music together. For me this was a very happy time. The number of music pupils was on the increase, the introduction of GCSE had made music much more accessible as a classroom subject, the whole-school music tradition was maintained and the School flourished. Probably the Quatercentenary year had the grandest musical event of my time at the School – the Barbican Concert. This was a celebration of all that is good about music at Aldenham, a balance between the best individual performers and whole-school music; it was a truly memorable evening. It presented the School with a unique opportunity and I think we took it – we fulfilled our potential in a big way!

The stimulating musical environment at Aldenham also provided inspiration for Nicholas Yates (SH 1986–91), who was subsequently a choral scholar at Cambridge, and who writes: *During my time at Aldenham (1986–1991) the School was fortunate enough to have at the musical helm two extremely good music teachers: Alan Vening, who was the Director of Music, and Geoffrey Barker.*

Geoffrey had the great misfortune of teaching me the violin, an instrument which I enjoyed, but one on which I struggled to get beyond being merely acceptable. This was no reflection of his teaching ability, but simply that my endeavours to rival the great violin luminaries were increasingly overshadowed by my aptitude at singing, something I could do much better and with much less practice.

At School, Alan Vening was wholly responsible for encouraging me to sing and he would use his great gift on the ivories to make that all the more rewarding. He was a keyboardist par excellence, but especially on his beloved piano. He would accompany me as we worked our way through all kinds of repertoire: Lieder, French songs, as well as the 20th-century English repertoire. He was always willing and able to transpose anything at sight into a more suitable key for a young voice (and often into a very difficult key).

In fact, Alan Vening achieved a rare feat as a music teacher in that he was, more or less, universally loved by the whole School. His continuation of the public school tradition of the entire School singing together at concerts, well beyond its sell-by date in

other such schools, was visionary and extraordinary and but one of my memories of my musical life at Aldenham. I can remember with great fondness mainframe choral repertoire, such as Handel's 'Hallelujah' chorus (from Messiah) and Verdi's 'Chorus of the Hebrew Slaves' (from Nabucco), being arranged by him to enable everyone in the School to sing. Haydn's Creation was also another highlight, in which I sang the tenor solos just before I left the School. These concerts were only outshone by the corporate, and often repeated, rendition of Alan's own Christmas carol, To Hunt the Wren.

My abiding recollection of my musical and, to some extent, my academic life at Aldenham was the encouragement and inspiration provided by those who taught me. Inspiration did not, of course, exude from every area of School life, but it did most certainly from the Music and Theology Departments, and I have the then Chaplain, Simon Bloxam-Rose, to thank for the latter. We also had immense fun.

All of this, and, of course, much hard work, led to me gaining a place at Trinity College, Cambridge, to read Theology, together with a choral scholarship. During my time in the choir at Trinity under

Dr Richard Marlow I went on over 20 international tours and made over 15 CDs. It was a defining three years for me and one that I would not have been able to reach and harness were it not for the skills that Aldenham had bequeathed to me: independence of thought, an ability to empathise with others and, most importantly, confidence.

It is precisely those attributes that I now use constantly in my working life at the bar, and it is no exaggeration to say that without the galvanisation that Aldenham provided, things may have turned out very differently.

John Wyatt (Director of Music from 1994) describes how the musical life of the School has developed in recent years with the opening of the new Music School in 2000 and the transformation of the House Music Competition into a major annual event: *A major change to the House Music Competition was to invite parents to watch. This meant that the small hall, which was going to be converted into a new theatre anyway, was too small for such an event. Two options were available if the competition was to stay on the site of the School. One was the Chapel, which seemed not very practical and still rather small, or the Sports Hall. The second venue became the favoured choice and since 2006, the Sports Hall has been transformed into a concert venue with the* addition of curtains around the walls, a lighting rig, a stage, amplification and the hire of a concert grand piano. The House Music Competition is now one of the highlights of the year, with an audience of about 1,200 pupils and parents.

In 2000 Dame Janet Baker opened the new Music School. This has allowed the School to increase the capacity of individual music lessons, which usually range between 170 and 200 lessons taught by 19 visiting staff each week. The class lessons are taught in a classroom equipped with new Apple Mac computers by two full-time staff. There is also one part-time member of staff specialising in A level Music Technology and a part-time secretary. The new building also contains a beautiful recital room, several practice rooms, a recording studio and recently a harp has been donated to the department and lessons for this started in October 2010.

Over the past few years the department has also embarked on taking various groups out to perform. This has included visits to sing Evensong at Winchester and Lichfield cathedrals, the college chapels of Clare, Emmanuel and Corpus Christi Cambridge, and Exeter and Wadham in Oxford. Concerts have also been given in the church of Great St Mary, Cambridge and abroad in Notre Dame, Brussels Cathedral, Cologne Cathedral, St George's Memorial Church, Ypres and other venues in France, Germany and Holland. The Carol Service is also now regularly held at St Albans Cathedral to allow for the increased number of parents who like to attend.

Left: Boys singing in the unison section of the House Music Competition, 2008.

Below: Verity Gosden (P 2007–9) participating in the 2007 House Music competition.

Ascent *(oil on linen)*
by Simon Boyd
(K 1992–7).

ART

Art has always flourished at Aldenham. When he was a pupil at the School in the 1990s, Simon Boyd (K 1992–7), now a professional artist, described his 'view of art' in *The Aldenhamian*: *To talk about Art is invariably an impossible task because of its versatility as a subject. It is personal to the artist and, although one may be influenced by outside sources, it is up to him to lay down the paint. Because of this personal aspect, there is so much to be explored and discovered by the individual. Indeed, this freedom of expression is one of the central attractions of art.*

There are no fixed methods or restrictions by formula, and so art is able to conform to the ambiguities and complications resonant with human nature. Art is a set of definitive statements that cannot be questioned or scrutinised; it is final and exists in its own right. As an artist, I think it is essential to be prepared to take risks in order to develop through a series of discoveries. There is a tendency in observational work to tighten up; art should be a freeing experience, an expression which doesn't have to correlate exactly to reality, but has some personal identity…

Art for me is a catharsis of the spirit; not only does it give satisfaction and provoke a general realisation, but it makes me happy.

In 2010, he writes that: *…it's strange, looking back at an article I wrote in 1996, to consider how much of what I wrote as a 17-year-old is still relevant to my current practice as a painter…*

My painting has always been about taking risks; to be as free and open as possible. For me painting is a slow and awkward process, without a distinctive start and finish. It is a series of experiments initiated through trial and error.

Over the past couple of years I have slowed down my productive output, preferring to allow my work to gradually mature of its own accord. I have learnt to appreciate the experience of the journey, rather than rushing the process to get to a particular destination or conclusion. In this sense my painting has become

Left: Paul Spencer
has been teaching
Pottery since 1985.

Below left: Deduced
by Peter McDonald
(M 1986–91)
2007. From a
series of paintings of
teachers teaching. Kate
MacGarry Gallery.

Right: Serious
concentration in the
Pre-Prep.

more personal, more organic on many levels, a liberating mixture of abstraction and realism...

I am currently living in Argentina and have recently enjoyed a solo exhibition at The British Arts Centre, Buenos Aires, in November 2009, and will be exhibiting in Miami this December at the Red Dot Art Fair ... The years I spent at Aldenham helped me to grow as a person and as an artist. I don't forget that.

Peter McDonald (M 1986–91), winner of the John Moores Painting Prize in 2008, is another Aldenhamian who has developed a career as a painter. He recalls: I was sure I wanted to do something artistic. The Art Department I remember was a refuge for me from the regime of the School day. It was where I could experiment with ideas, listen to music and generally play around with all the materials available. I think in retrospect the freedom that was encouraged in the Art Department at that time makes me very grateful for that space ... I now have a studio and a gallery in London where I am painting everyday.

My paintings depict a colourful world inhabited by people engaged in everyday activities. Images of teachers, scientists or hairdressers are constructed with an elementary graphic language. Human forms veer towards the geometric: circles stand in for heads, flat planes describe rooms and crude poses denote narrative. Yet these simplifications appear to create a community of superhumans living in a world that has a harmonious transparency. By making use of archetypes, symbolism and our irresistible tendency to make the strange readable, this alternative world operates like a parallel universe. This utopia may be a vision of an ideal world in the future or a simplified and optimistic version of the one we already know...

OUR
COSMOS

TEN COMMANDMENTS
The Sweet Heaven

MILL
Lydia
4118

DEVELOPMENT

OBSERVATION

BANKSY

DEVELOPMENT 2

DEVELOPMENT 2

THE SCHOOL LIBRARY

The School Library dominates the landscape at Aldenham. It is also a major focus for learning in the School and was presided over for 20 years by Sara Price (Librarian 1986–2006), the School's first professionally trained Librarian: *The School Library has been physically in the centre of Aldenham School since it was built as a memorial to those pupils who died in the First World War. It was opened in 1924 and the Librarian for the next 40 years was Cecil Stott. It was entirely thanks to his vision that the collection became as diverse and all-encompassing as it remains. Two equally erudite men followed him: Bernard Gordon and David Wallace-Hadrill, each of whom ran the Library for ten years, before I took over for the next 20 years.*

The Library did not remain static. Originally a free standing building at the end of the Shed, it expanded into it in 1979, creating a Careers Library and offices for the Librarian and the Careers Master. In 2005 it was linked to the Richard Platt building, which replaced the Shed when there was a need for new classrooms. Inside, the Library also underwent several changes. Initially the bulk of the book stock had been geared to the more classical subjects with a large theology section, history, English and foreign plays and poetry, as well as an ever-expanding Reference section. As new subjects were introduced, new material was collected – economics, business studies, sports science and drama all being areas which expanded rapidly.

With the rise in Information Technology, not only were books added to the collection but computers also made their way into the Library. At first there were three machines for student use which were kept in the store room which had previously housed incunabula (much of which was sold in the 1990s), and one for the Librarian's use in the office … In due course the upper floor of the Library was equipped with a number of PCs, with one in each of the bays and several in the Stott Room. It was important that there remained an area of quiet, so that students who wished to read and work were given priority on the ground floor.

The Library remains at the centre of School life. It hosts receptions, meetings and other events and provides a showcase for the success of the School and the achievements of its pupils. It is a major part of that 'foundation for success'.

chapter seven

Horizons

Although for most of its history Aldenham has been somewhat isolated, in recent decades it has increasingly engaged with the local community and with the wider world. This engagement started in the early years of the 20th century with the work of the Aldenham Boys' Club in Kentish Town.

This engagement increased as the School made contact with local Primary Schools, Care Homes for Senior Citizens and Day Centres for the Mentally Handicapped, and as pupils made regular visits to support teachers in the classroom, to visit those who lived on their own and to join in with activities designed to stimulate those with learning difficulties. Many a pupil who found the discipline of School life irksome was seen to flourish in this very different environment. Former pupils have looked back on this as a formative experience.

Horizons were further extended as pupils took advantage of one of the most ambitious schemes of Careers Education in the Independent sector. Fifth Form aptitude tests have been used for many years and continue to provide advice and guidance on Sixth Form subjects, university courses and career options. Work Experience was, and is, an integral part of the Lower Sixth programme and provides opportunities in this country and abroad.

With the advent of Aldenham School Enterprises, the commercial arm of the School, with the arrival of Camp Aldenham, the children's holiday club, and with the building of the Sports Hall, more and more local people were introduced to the School and its facilities. These facilities were hired out to local clubs and societies, and the England Hockey Team was just one of the many groups that found the Sports Hall a suitable and convenient venue for team practice.

SERVICE
Aldenham Boys' Club
Since 1911, the School had supported the Aldenham Boys' Club in Kentish Town. The club flourished in the early decades of the century, and close links were established between the club and the School. In later years, however, it became increasingly difficult to find good leaders and to secure financial support, and the club was closed in 1985. Peter Boorman (Headmaster 1974–83) has described the efforts that were made to obtain grants, and pays tribute to

John Woodrow, who worked tirelessly to keep the club open: *Ex-officio I found myself Chairman of the Boys' Club in 1974, though in part responding to the call of John, who was Secretary. The call was persuasive to say the least, coming from one who was so committed. John had been Secretary for some years and had seen the club struggle to maintain activities in the midst of difficult, largely financial, restraints. Those with any knowledge of the politics and economics of that time will know that problems pre-1974 were nothing compared to the turbulent years that followed. These problems created special difficulties for the club...*

When Mrs Thatcher came to power the deficit grants stopped. Any plans we presented had to be properly and formally documented with surveyors' and architects' plans, leading to inevitable delays. No longer could we put in a bottom line figure leaving us a little over to spend on the young people. As the profligacy of the early 1970s became market forces in the late 1970s, the Aldenham Boys' Club suffered very badly. Throughout this whole period John's work was the nearest thing to altruism I have ever seen.

Community Service

The diversification of Friday afternoon activities into 'service activities' in the local community and in the School itself saved the notion of a 'service' afternoon from extinction. The Voluntary Service Unit encouraged groups of boys to visit residential homes for the elderly and day centres for the mentally handicapped. They also helped out at Gills Hill Infants' School, Sandy Lane Travellers' Site and

Above: Visitors from Crossroads - a Senior Citizen's Day Centre in Borehamwood - are entertained every Thursday at the School for lunch.

Below left: The Aldenham Boys' Club in the 1960s.

the Watford Day Nursery. They paid regular visits to the housebound to help with shopping or to cut the lawn. These visits were well supported by the pupils and much appreciated by those whom they helped. It was often those boys who were most disruptive in School who came to be the most productive in these relationships. To observe boys engaging with these elderly people was a salutary experience.

Community service activities within the School itself were an important part of the overall scheme. House Maintenance groups, Estate Work teams and the Nature Conservancy group involved boys in caring for the buildings, fabric and grounds of the School. The Forestry group, for example, was very active during the Dutch Elm Disease outbreak. Routine work was the main part of the job, but some impressive projects were also completed. Although it was difficult at times to maintain the 'service' element in the Friday afternoon scheme, as some activities strayed from this norm, it was nevertheless a time in which many boys found real fulfilment.

Community service extended to the support of a variety of different charities over the years, most notably through sponsorship of the Eros Run and in the recent commitment to Ripple Africa.

The Eros Run

Terry Ford (CR 1979 onwards), who has organised the run in recent years, describes the initial inspiration and subsequent history of this major School event: *Sir Alfred Gilbert (1854–1934) was a pupil at the School from 1865 to 1872. During that time, his talents as an artist became very evident, as can be seen from the carving in terracotta he produced in 1870 of his*

Headmaster, Revd Alfred Leeman, which is currently on display in the Library. After leaving the School, one of his commissions was to produce the statue for Piccadilly Circus, usually, if erroneously, known as Eros (Gilbert himself indicated it was Anteros, the younger brother of Eros, symbolising creative and selfless love), which commemorates the life and works of the Earl of Shaftesbury, the great Victorian social reformer perhaps best known for major improvements like the Climbing Boys Act. In designing the statue, he produced small-scale models or maquettes, one of which was in the Tate Gallery. In 1949, exceptional permission was granted for a casting to be made and this was erected in the newly created war memorial garden behind the Library, just beyond the window graced by his statue of Leeman.

In 1977, J ('Chemical Jim') Robinson instituted a charity run from Piccadilly Circus to the School on the last morning of the summer term – called, not surprisingly, the Eros-to-Eros Run. To avoid rush-hour traffic, it starts at 5am and essentially follows Edgware Road back to the School. Sadly, the School's example of Eros was stolen in 1978. Thankfully, a further casting has been allowed and this replacement was put in position in 1984. In addition, for a while the statue in Piccadilly was removed for restoration, so, although the run has taken place every year, it has been variously, Eros to Eros, Eros to where Eros was, from where Eros was to where Eros was and now, finally, again Eros to Eros.

The run has become a well-established tradition of the School, but the number of participants has varied considerably. Usually there are about 25 to 30 pupils, staff, OAs and friends of the School, but there was one year in which 85 took part. The one constant factor has been the generosity of the sponsors of the runners, it being not unusual for individuals to go into three figures with their sponsorship. Charities supported have ranged from the local, such as Watford New Hope Trust, which cares for the homeless of Watford, through the national, such as the Royal National Institute for the Blind, to the international, such as Ripple Africa.

Ripple Africa

In 2003, Geoff Furber (SH 1970–4) and his wife, Liz, purchased a property on the northern shores of Lake Malawi and started a charity called Ripple Africa, which is involved with education, healthcare, and environmental projects. Ripple Africa's philosophy is to provide a hand up and not a hand out by helping the local people to help themselves. Geoff: *In 2008, when Dan Bond, the Aldenham School Chaplain, found out about the charity, he asked me to give a talk at the School. Since then, Aldenham has been regularly supporting the work that Ripple Africa is*

doing. To date, the School has sent out three groups of students and teachers who, after going on safari in Zambia, have spent two weeks staying at Ripple Africa's Lowani Beach. They have been involved with many of the projects that Ripple Africa is working on and have experienced the local culture. The students have assisted with building a community clinic, a teacher's house, a primary school classroom block, and with repairing the house of a local HIV sufferer. Some have also helped with teaching, worked in the tree nursery and learnt about deforestation, healthcare and local agriculture.

The School has been very supportive and has hosted a number of fundraising events which have not only raised money but have also raised awareness of what rural life is like in sub-Saharan Africa. The students who have been lucky enough to visit Malawi with the School have seen at first hand how hard day-to-day life is for rural Malawians, but they have been inspired by how happy the people are although they have so little.

Merchant Vessel *Glenartney*

In 1941 Aldenham adopted the MV *Glenartney* as part of the Ship Adoption Scheme. Martin Field (CR 1989–2005) describes the recent resurgence of interest in this link: *During the war when Glenartney was taking part in many a perilous convoy, not least the famous Malta convoy or, due to her speed, sailing on her own without escort, correspondence flowed between pupils and crew, though as GB Smethurst (P 1944–8)* recalls, 'Heaven knows what they made of what we had to say!' Captain Jerry Lawton, who was then a midshipman on *Glenartney*, echoed this sentiment. He later wrote to Aldenham pupils that 'because one could not write of destinations, voyages, or even cargoes, much time was spent chewing the end of the pen for ideas!' Many assemblies were also full of stories and news of *Glenartney*'s endeavours. After the war, having survived with a very distinguished record, *Glenartney* played host to many an Aldenham party.

Research in 1995 led to much documentary evidence of the link. Amongst the letters, drawings, fine wartime paintings and general memorabilia, a model of *Glenartney* purported to have been made by David Wallace-Hadrill (CR 1950–5, 1962–86) and a framed navigational chart presented to Aldenham by Captain Evans in 1946 were found in the School. This research and the interest it created led to an exhibition and a Commemoration Service held in the Chapel. The highlights of the beautiful and moving service, which linked the generations by bringing together present pupils and staff, Old Aldenhamians and seamen of the ship, were to have the sermon delivered by Canon Peter Ball (B 1944–8), who had as a boy visited *Glenartney*, and to have the large congregation witness a memorial plaque being unveiled.

The Glenartney Memorial in the School Chapel.

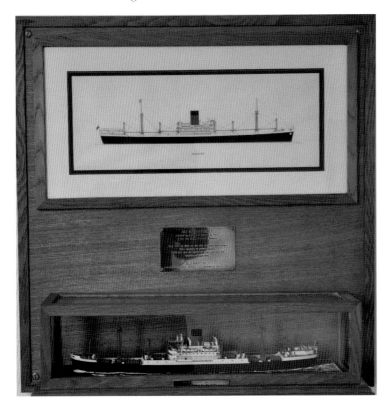

As one of the *Glenartney* generation said 'I think it made us all very proud that Aldenham School has seen fit to revive its interest in *Glenartney* and commemorate in such a fine manner her service and that of the men who sailed in her'.

CAREERS

Aldenham was in the forefront of Careers Education from the early 1970s, and led the way in a number of important initiatives under the direction of Robert Stokes. The weekly visits from those in industry, commerce and the professions gave Sixth Form pupils an opportunity to find out about a range of careers, and the annual industrial conference enabled them to participate in games, simulations and debates with young managers from an equally wide range of companies. In due course a scheme of regular visits to companies and institutions was organised in the Summer Term.

Work experience became an established part of the Lower Sixth programme for all boys and girls from the 1980s. For one week at the beginning of the Spring Term, all members of the Lower Sixth spent a week of work experience with companies in the local area and in London. The School arranged all placements. Some pupils also travelled further afield, and each year a small number was placed with companies in France, Germany or Belgium, with the help of the Radlett town-twinning scheme and Rotary International. In 1991, Aldenham School's European Work Experience programme won an award from the Hertfordshire Technician Education Council.

The Careers Department was also active with other groups. The use of tests and interviews to help parents and Fifth Form boys and girls to gain an objective view of strengths and weaknesses, and to offer advice on academic choices and career options, was pioneered in schools such as Aldenham. The School had close links with the Independent Schools Careers Organisation and used a battery of tests administered by them. The relatively wide range of ability of pupils at Aldenham meant that advice and guidance at the Fifth Form stage was crucial. Both pupils and parents needed help in making choices of A level subjects and in exploring possibilities for the future.

In the Upper Sixth Form year, all pupils were given help with the plans for university entrance and the completion of UCAS forms. It was not always easy to persuade pupils and their parents to be realistic. When results were published during the summer holidays, members of staff were on hand to give support for at least the following three weeks. Again, the wide range of grades achieved meant that some pupils needed help to find alternative courses and institutions. 'Gap' years were popular with Aldenham pupils and were encouraged if they had been well researched and planned.

Careers work continues to flourish at Aldenham and there have been some amusing incidents as pupils have been let loose into the real world, as Howard Dymock (Careers Master 1993–2002) explains: *On one occasion I visited a pair of Sixth Formers doing their week of work experience with the Metropolitan Police. Although Radlett police station was possibly the quietest posting in the force, Dennis, the well-known local personality of the era, took great pride in organising a varied week. On this occasion it included the boys having to sit on a suspect apprehended in Borehamwood, and lend the coppers ten pence for a coin box telephone to summon assistance, since their radios had failed. Among visits to the dog and horse sections, I muscled in on an evening trip to the riot-training centre in Hounslow. Five of us piled into the local Austin Metro police car, which sank so low on its springs that it frequently grounded, and crawled towards Heathrow. The boys took great delight in the slow-moving traffic in leaning out of the windows to spot any neighbouring cars with expired tax discs, and a record clutch of tickets were issued on the A4 that night. However, the real fun was donning protective fireproof clothing, and then running around a mock urban landscape, lighting Molotov cocktails in milk bottles and flinging them with impunity at real police officers undergoing training. This was, of course, before today's Health and Safety culture!*

On another day, when the Brewers had generously sponsored and organised a day in the garden of a pub in Greenford, patrons were rather surprised to see 80 Sixth Formers in groups in the large garden, solving a variety of tasks. After welcome hospitality at lunchtime, sandwiches and beer, the final challenge was for each group to set off a firework without going within a certain distance of it, utilising certain items supplied. Eventually some cottoned on to how to achieve this, and the area soon began to buzz with motorised Lego vehicles holding lighted splints, pulleys and guide ropes, and then resounded to the bang of fireworks. Unhappily it coincided with a time of terrorist alerts in the capital, and a local resident contacted the police. Just as we were packing up,

Bob Collins (Careers Master from 2003) giving advice to pupils in the Careers Room.

Work experience: Masuma Ashikaki (B 2001–3) with a fashion design company in 2002; Edward Barton-Hilton (B 2000–5) in an engineering company; Rubel Mallik (B 1996–03) in a fish market in 2002; Neil Shah (M 1996–8) with a dentist in 1997.

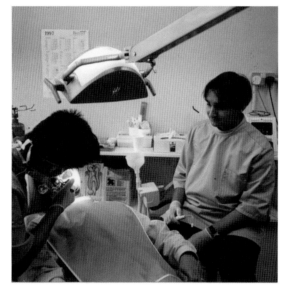

armed officers surrounded the premises, pointing their sub-machine guns threateningly at us all, and some explaining had to be done.

Work experience took place in a variety of companies and organisations both in the UK and abroad. Alex Twitchell (P 1986–91) gives an account of his week in the Hermès store in Paris: *For my work experience I was placed in Hermès, a luxury goods store known worldwide, on the prestigious Rue du Faubourg Saint-Honoré in the centre of Paris. This wonderful opportunity was arranged via the Twinning Committee of Radlett and Louveciennes, a town just to the west of Paris itself, and also thanks to the hard work of the Mayor of Louveciennes.*

On the first day at Hermès I was taken on a tour of the entire shop by Monsieur Herlony, who showed me all the various departments – from ready-to-wear and perfumes to leather goods and jewellery.

I met during this tour all the heads of the various departments and by mid-morning I was working in la rayon des textiles. This department, headed by Mme la Compère and assisted by Letitia and Sophie, sold mainly porcelain, bath and beach towels, cashmere scarves, and luxury picnic items (especially with hunting in mind). I found that I had to learn prices very quickly, as customers expected one to know these things straight away!

The next afternoon I worked with jewellery, watches, brooches and so on, guided by Eric, a quite young salesman fluent in English, who left me to wander about with the keys to the display racks. However, I felt it was not such a good idea to open up these racks to look at the items, so I left them firmly shut! It was also explained how the friendlier atmosphere and a far more personal relationship with the client were so important in the jewellery department, as was greatly evident.

The following day I was placed in the carrés (squares, normally in silk) department, world famous and probably the busiest in the entire store! I was given a lightning introduction to all the serveuses, at least ten or so in all, and was then shown all the squares in their respective colours and designs: this was not easy to memorise at once! Luckily for me the lady in charge was very patient. The day was very frantic and haphazard …

This placement was different from anything I had ever done before in my life. Not only was it because I was speaking French the entire day, or because of the prices, but also because of the generally friendly atmosphere of a large store such as Hermès. I recognised immediately the traditional and family-like atmosphere, and felt at home …

137

SUPPORT

Over the years, many individuals and organisations have supported the School. These have included the Aldenham School Parents' Association (ASPA), The Old Aldenhamian Society, The Friends of Aldenham School and the Brewers' Company. Aldenham School Enterprises, the School's commercial arm, has also played a key role, not least in running Camp Aldenham over many years.

The Aldenham School Parents' Association (ASPA)

John McAllister (CR 1967–2005), who was instrumental in the founding of the Parents' Association, describes its success: *To any headmaster in the 1980s, the prospect of a parents' association was positive anathema, conjuring up haunting images of unsolicited parental interference. Nevertheless, and after the idea had been mooted to his predecessor, Michael Higginbottom agreed to allow a Parents' Association at Aldenham.*

ASPA was formed essentially to act as a social forum for Aldenhamian Parents. Fortunate in the experience and enthusiasm of its early committees and further strengthened by the tremendous drive and support of the Headmaster's wife, the Association launched into unchartered waters. In the early years the Association held regular termly events; quiz evenings, champagne tasting and Barn Dances all attracted capacity crowds, not least because of a wonderful succession of gourmet experts on the committee. Confidence grew and ASPA staged its first Ball. The rest is history.

There can be no doubt that the friendships formed in the early years, not just within the committee but as importantly amongst all participating parents, exceeded all expectations and the School inevitably gained from the friendships thus formed. The 1990s were not necessarily easy times for the School, but the goodwill generated by the activities of ASPA provided a very real source of strength. That goodwill remains but is, as yet, undeveloped and there is surely scope for a Former ASPA. Two attempts at Reunion Dinners were well received and attended and that avenue could well merit further research.

The Brewers' Company

The Brewers' Company has also been a major supporter of the School since its foundation. In February 1596 Richard Platt obtained Letters Patent from Queen Elizabeth I, which permitted him to build 'The Free Grammar School of Richard Platte' at Aldenham. The Governing Body was to be the 'Master Wardens and Cominaltie of the Mysterie or Arte of Brewers of the Citie of London', thus beginning the long and happy relationship of the School and the Company. Without the Company there would be no School; its members alone were Governors until the 20th century and only in 1995 was a non-Brewer Chairman appointed for the first time; the freehold of the School was not transferred to the Aldenham School Charity from the Company until 1996. The Company has given substantial financial support at various stages of the School's history, while individual Brewers have been notably generous.

Each year the new Third Form (Year 9s) are invited to Brewers' Hall in the City of London for the Beer Money ceremony. Tim Lello (CR 1998–2001) describes the scene: *As the Master and members of the Worshipful Company of Brewers entered in all their finery, there was a real sense of occasion and a feeling that we were taking part in an historical event. We were entertained by the Master's speech explaining the connection between the Brewers and the School from its earliest Tudor foundation, and the boys were presented with a commemorative £5 coin, the first of its kind to be minted for the new*

Left: The Master of the Brewers' Company, accompanied by the Beadle, presents Beer Money to a Year 9 pupil.

The Old Aldenhamian Society

Neil Sutherland, President of the Society writes:

Much has been written about the role of old boys'/old girls' societies in English public schools and the demise of 'the old school tie' in providing an automatic entrance to elite business or social institutions. Yet this shallow interpretation of the value of such societies does little justice to the natural wish of many Old Aldenhamians to remain in touch with fellow pupils, to be able to meet and catch up on common reminiscences of youth and to forge closer bonds between those who have shared a common education and whose lives have been enhanced by the Aldenham ethos.

The original aims of the OA Society, formed in April 1902, in the Freemason's Tavern, Great Queen Street, London, remain delivered to this day – a register of OAs; good communications between Aldenham School and OAs, and between OAs themselves; an annual edition of the Aldenhamiana *magazine; an Old Aldenhamian dinner 'from time to time' and united action through an elected committee. The final aim is to further the interests of the School and of present and past members 'in such ways as from time to time may be possible'.*

The most notable achievement of the OA Society in helping the School can be seen in the construction of the School Library as a War Memorial in 1923; 163 OAs and masters lost their lives in the First World War. While there have been many contributions since, the OA Society as a whole, and its individual members, continue to be most generous in all appeals, such as providing the replacement Eros in 1985, making major contributions to the new School Theatre and the recent gift of a harp. The Society also provides an annual Travel Scholarship to the School.

Today's OA Society is a vibrant and active organisation, dedicated to the service of OAs and fully supporting the School in all its endeavours. Modern media are now used for much of our communications and new ways have been developed to enhance the aim of fostering friendship and improving the contact between former pupils. The interest shown in OA Day attendance has blossomed since the 'house gaudy' initiative, while other examples are the Aldenham.net informal networking meetings in London, regional lunches and dinners held across UK and in other countries (Malaysia and Singapore in 2010). In the future we will also be exploring new ways of fostering friendship, such as through social media and the introduction of a business mentoring scheme for new OAs in the early years of their chosen careers. OAs will continue to contribute to the life of the School through supporting new appeals and also by providing a natural channel for sporting talent to move into once School days are over.

From the top: OAs were major contributers towards the purchase of a harp played in this photograph by Alastair Heald (M 2008–); OA Annual Dinner, 2008; OA Reunion, 1946.

millennium. There was regret that one of the School's old traditions of having a regular pint of beer for breakfast no longer happens, and fascination in the documents shown to us by the Archivist, including an exquisite and rarely seen portrait of Elizabeth I.

As the final part of the Quatercentenary celebrations a stained glass window, based on a design by junior pupils and incorporating the coats of arms of the Whitbread and Martineau families (long associated with the School), was dedicated in the Aldenham School Chapel on 30 April 1999. The Letchmore Trust funded the window.

The Friends of Aldenham School

In the early 1950s, a small group of dedicated OAs formed The Friends of Aldenham School Association (The Friends), a company limited by guarantee, which has charitable status. For 20 years the Friends actively supported School projects including, among other gifts, the Football stand, the Art Block and Sixth Form Common Room. There followed a period of hibernation as the main role of The Friends had been absorbed by the Aldenham School General Charitable Trust. Today The Friends continue to make donations to the School; however these are now smaller, reflecting the loss of membership over the years.

The Letchmore Trust

The Letchmore Trust is a registered charity that was created in 1958, primarily with the object of holding on trust various paintings (particularly *The Crucifixion* by Sir Stanley Spencer, which hung in the Chapel). The paintings, which comprised most of the assets of the Trust, were sold in 1990 and the majority of the cash proceeds were gifted to the School. Since then, the balance of the proceeds has been held in quoted investments as a Trust Fund for general charitable purposes. The policy of the Trustees is to use the income arising from the investments to commission works of art to be gifted to and/or displayed at Aldenham School, or for other purposes related to the arts.

The Aldenham School War Memorial Educational Fund

The Fund is a registered charity that was created in 1947 to assist financially in the education of the sons of Old Aldenhamians and others who had died or otherwise suffered as a result of the Second World War, and for wider charitable purposes that the Trustees may consider beneficial to the School's pupils. In 1987 the definition of those who may benefit was widened to include girls.

Above: The stained glass window incorporating the coats of arms of the Whitbread and Martineau families in the Chapel.

Left: Members of the Whitbread family, together with Stephen Borthwick and Bishop Peter Dawes (M 1941–6) at the dedication of the Brewers' Window in the Chapel in 1999.

Aldenham School Enterprises (ASE)

Aldenham School Enterprises was started in 1982 as the commercial arm of Aldenham School. David Mead, the General Manager up until 2010, was the driving force of the organisation. ASE was responsible for managing a number of important ventures that made a considerable contribution to School life over the years, including Camp Aldenham, the Sports Hall and the School Shop. The Nursery School, opened in 1992 in the Cricket Pavilion under the leadership of Jan Harris, was a notable success. ASE also handled lettings for functions, film and TV productions as well as activities for children, such as theatre and soccer coaching and a Language School. These functions were an important showcase for the School.

Camp Aldenham

Camp Aldenham ran from 1981 to 2008. It not only provided income for the School, but also raised its profile in the local community and provided an introduction to the School for those who subsequently joined as pupils. Cyril Tyson (1952–87), who created Camp Aldenham and was its first Director, wrote about the scheme in *The Aldenhamian* of 1985: *Camp Aldenham has now become a regular feature in the Aldenham School year. In 1984, our well-established multi-activity camp ran for five separate weeks, Monday to Friday, until August 24th. During that time we had over 1,450 children (280+ each week) enjoying every moment of their day which started at 9.30am and ended at 4.30pm. Many of the monitors were back for their third year, so much do they enjoy it, too, and many of the children, aged 5 to 13, were returning for their third successive year and not merely staying for one week, but for two, or even more! We enjoyed a fine summer, with rain on our first day, and torrential rain on the last Friday afternoon to close the Camp, but between times we only had the odd shower and there was little interference with the planned outdoor activities.*

In 1985 we shall be opening on July 22nd – again for five weeks, Monday to Friday – and the Camp will close on August 23rd. We shall be introducing Go-Karting for the first time, but we shall also have a sensational 'first': we are giving the oldest children an opportunity to fly! In conjunction with Cabair and the London School of Flying at Elstree Airfield, we are offering a half-day Introduction to Flying, during the course of which three children at a time will be given one hour's flying instruction in a dual-controlled plane with a flying instructor, with each child having 20 minutes at the controls. So far as we know, no other Camp in the country is offering such an exciting feature.

DEVELOPMENT

Following research by an outside Marketing Agency, Jones Knowles Ritchie was appointed to come up with proposals for the development of the marketing function at Aldenham. A Marketing Department was set up in August 1992 to encourage more enquiries to the School and convert them into new pupils, both day and boarding. This included looking in particular at the overseas market and increasing the number of girls at the School. Heather Sherman (Marketing Manager from 2001) continues the story: *Jane Britton joined as the first Marketing Manager in 1992, a role that had previously been undertaken by Richard Wood. This turned out to be an important element to the future success of the School's fortunes; focusing on image building, targeted advertising, improving recording systems and contact with feeder schools. Along with other independent schools, it was essential for Aldenham to be seen to be delivering customer satisfaction, excellent service and value for money. A new prospectus was commissioned, and regular newsletters and Open Days were established. When Jane left a year later to have her twins, Helen Elliott fulfilled this role until Jane's return as Marketing Director in 1995. When Jane moved to Epsom College, I succeeded her. Numbers, which had fallen to 316 in 1983 and were still only 326 in 1992, gradually began to rise (381 in 1996). Today the total School population, including the Prep School, is a very healthy 700 boys and girls.*

Molly Barton, the first Development Manager at the School, joined in 2001 and immediately set about building good relationships with alumni and ensuring that an accurate database was established. The first major challenge the Development Office tackled was a fundraising campaign for the new Theatre. Old Aldenhamians, parents, Governors and others connected to the School donated £300,000 towards the cost. The Aldenham Annual Fund, launched in 2008, raises money for projects that have an immediate impact on the School. Items the fund has already provided include cricket covers, a harp, two

Prep School children at work and play.

Firefly dinghies, new Library chairs and numerous smaller items in every part of the School. Numerous OA Days, Gaudys, Regional Lunches and Music Recitals have all ensured that OAs are able to keep in touch with their old School and with each other.

The Junior School evolved in stages over a number of years, starting with the Nursery School in 1992, Martineau's House in 1993, the Pre-Prep in 2000 and the Preparatory School in 2003. The Junior and Senior parts of the School now cater for boys and girls of all ages from three to 18. Kate Watts (Head of Foundation Stage and Deputy Head of Prep School), Martin Langston (Housemaster Martineau's House 1996–2004) and Paul Cheetham (Headmaster Prep School 2003–7) describe this evolution: *Aldenham Nursery School was the brainchild of David Mead and Aldenham School Enterprises over 18 years ago. Under the dynamic leadership of Jan Harris the Nursery first opened its doors to three staff children, including her own son,*

in September 1992. Situated in the Cricket Pavilion, on Top Field, each day the equipment had to be set up and then cleared away again.

Within months its reputation had grown and the Nursery was vibrant and busy. Before long it had outgrown the Pavilion and needed bigger, more permanent premises. In November 1993 Wilson House (the old School sanatorium) was to be the new venue and the business thrived. Jan remembers this being 'a period of great excitement, rapid growth and new found achievement'. Never short of pupils, the Nursery established itself as one of the most sought after places to offer nursery education.

Our last OFSTED inspection, in June 2008 judged us as 'outstanding', something we are very proud of. Only 5 per cent of nurseries in the country can boast of such an achievement. Now in a permanent building we have two nursery classes (Elmer and Wilbur) and offer sessions or full day places; many children attend five full days. Before Pre-Prep opened, all children were leaving for other local schools. At the time, along with parental pressure, Governors had the vision to grow the Nursery into a Pre-Prep. Builders worked all summer to refurbish the old Music School in Wilson House

into the first classroom and in September 2000 it opened its doors to 16 pupils in new uniforms ready to start their school careers …

Kate Watts

Mick Jonas made a start at building a strong educational foundation and bridging the gap between the end of primary stage and the traditional beginning of an Aldenham education at 13+. He had established the curriculum for the junior pupils and I felt my role was to build upon this and add some 'flesh to the bones' and focus on raising standards and expectations of the pupils in Martineau's.

Initially this involved developing a greater sense of belonging and we tried to borrow from the School's long and distinguished past to do this. We created four Houses, to reflect the strong House tradition of Aldenham and to allow for competition and responsibility for many pupils. The names of the Houses also linked to the School's past as former Headmasters Beck, Griffin, Neale and Mason became synonymous with Martineau's. This paved the way for a House Shield awarded to the highest achieving House on the sports field, in music, in drama, in grades and House points. Through intensive one-to-one tutoring each student was given support and help to maximise their start to secondary education at Aldenham. The tutor

team prided itself on the help and guidance it was able to give, and the intensity of the support given, and the care and dedication of the staff would be hard to match in any school in the country…

Martin Langston

The main charge of my new role was to oversee the bridging of the gap between the Foundation Stage and Pre-Prep and Martineau's House, by 'filling in' the missing years of 7 to 11. One of the attractions of joining the School in the early years was a clear route through to the Senior School and the possibility of a seamless education from 3 to 18.

So we started in the September of 2003 with a burgeoning Nursery, 35 children in the Pre-Prep, a brand new complement of 19 in the first year of the new Prep School and a lot of building, both physically and metaphorically to be done. It was not an auspicious first week, however, as we had to close the whole Prep School on the first Friday of term due to a lack of running water.

If I had to pick out the two most striking features of the Prep School, it would be the sense of community that was developed between all the stakeholders – parents, teachers and pupils – and just how happy the girls and boys generally were…

Paul Cheetham

BUILDINGS AND FACILITIES

Andrew Fraser (Bursar 1994–) outlines the development of buildings and facilities over the last two decades: *The decision in 1992 to offer education to 11- to 13-year-old boy pupils led to the opening of a newly constructed single-storey building named Martineau's House in 1993. In 1994 the conversion of one wing of Wilson House into Music teaching and practice rooms supplemented the facility in the Assembly/Drama Hall area. A rolling programme of refurbishment of classrooms and other parts of the School followed over several years.*

In 1996 the old School House changing rooms were converted into a new Design Technology Centre with an additional workshop constructed in an extension at the rear (financed by the Quatercentenary Appeal). The former Printing Room was converted into a second Information and Communication Technology laboratory. In the same year, a climbing wall was installed on the side wall of the Maths Block. This was financed by a bequest from the estate of Bernard Gordon.

In 1998 an artificial turf hockey surface with new floodlights on the site of the former Redgra pitch (funded from the Quatercentenary Appeal) was constructed and then opened by HRH The Princess Royal. The Old Chapel (also formally used as the Gymnasium and Design Technology Centre) was converted into the Music School (also funded by the Quatercentenary Appeal) in 1999–2000.

Aerial view of Aldenham School from the early 1920s.

The decision to open a Pre-Preparatory School for boys and girls led to the conversion of one wing of Wilson House (formally Music rooms) to Pre-Prep classrooms and the opening of the Aldenham Pre-Preparatory Department in September 2000, starting with a single Reception class and expanding by one year group each year. The decision to go further and open a Preparatory School, also for boys and girls, and to plan for co-education at all ages followed in 2001 and a two-storey extension to Martineau's House opened in January 2003. In 2003 the Near Old Block was converted into a day house for 11- to 13-year-old boys and girls with a fenced playground at the rear. The Martineau association with this group of pupils remained while the former building became wholly the Prep School and was renamed Woodrow House.

In the same year work then began on demolition of the former Games Shed to allow construction of a new classroom block and extension to the Masters' Common Room. The new block was completed in 2005 and named the Richard Platt Building. In 2007 there was major refurbishment of the Drama/Assembly Hall to form a purpose-built Theatre facility (partly funded through an Appeal) with Learning Support rooms at the rear.

In 2008 it was decided to expand the numbers in Martineau's House and to convert the ground floor of Kennedy's House to form a new day house and boarding facilities for boys and girls aged 11–13. A new playground/tennis/netball court was constructed. Martineau's House moved into Kennedy's House in September 2008. The Near Old Block returned to classroom use and the Near and Far Old Block were renamed Far Block.

In 2010 construction of a new Maintenance and Storage Building between Paull's House and the Artificial Pitch began (the first phase of a three-phase programme to create space for a Sixth Form Centre). The former maintenance building (previously the Armoury) was converted to re-house the School Shop and Centralised Purchasing, and to provide a new Music and Drama facility for the Prep School.

FUTURE PLANS

On my arrival as Headmaster in September 2006 I recognised that the most important future direction for the School had been set by the decision of the Governors at the beginning of the decade to move to full co-education throughout all years of the Senior School.

Within a very short time the wonderful complexities of life as a co-educational School became clear. The apparently innocent conjunction of a dance show and an overnight CCF camp on the same night created a real headache, with boys needing to perform in the dance show before a midnight dash to the camp and girls whose love for the CCF created conflict with their toe-tapping excellence in the theatre. In reality though it meant that some decisions were easy to take within a short space of time: Saturday school no longer became a feasible option since, if we had maintained it, girls would simply not have come to us; the decision to change the majority entry point for the Senior School from 13+ to 11+ meant that girls were much more likely to enter; we were able to relocate Martineau's to their new location on the ground floor of the Kennedy's building and provide for the very first time genuinely appropriate Junior boarding for girls and boys.

Above: Whole School photograph (2011), taken once every four years.

Right: Head Boy Tom Wainwright and first Head Girl Natasha Klimt (2010).

Possibly the most important factor that preserves the identity and style of the School, in a way which is cherished by parents and pupils alike, is the limit of 700 pupils being educated on the site. This limit, set by the local authority, was reached early in my time at the helm. We maintain as our clear focus the provision of the best possible education for these pupils. The creation of 'Vision 2013' to enhance the whole site and our facilities over the next few years is an exciting challenge.

At the heart of Vision 2013 will be a project to complete the space between the former Pavilion/Shop building and the Music School. This new building will provide an exceptional co-educational Sixth Form Centre, which can work in sympathy with the need for Sixth Formers also to lead their own Houses, as well as allowing us for the first time to open up the beautiful Recital Room for public performances with an appropriate foyer and reception area.

However, we also believe that the particular qualities of an Aldenham education should be available for a larger number of children and therefore from the beginning of 2011 we have been able to educate more children beyond our own site with our adoption of St Hilda's School, Bushey, into the Aldenham Foundation. In time it may be that the Aldenham brand, identified with consummate and

generous holistic education may reach other parts of the educational world. If it does so, the wishes of our founder to instil 'learning, knowledge and virtue' will be at the heart of the enterprise.

James Fowler

List of Subscribers

This book has been made possible through the generosity of the following subscribers:

IRS Abington	1955–9	Anthony Coote	2005–	Paul Griffin MBE	1962–74
Steve Adams	1952–6	Jamie Coote	2003–10	Dr Simon D J Griffin	1979–84
Timi Wayne Adeyanju	2010–	Claudio Corbetta	1989–91	Jasper Gruenewald	2003–10
Gerry Aird	1956–60	Graham Cornfield	1957–62	Geoffrey Gunton	1964–7
Richard Anderson	1953–7	Lester Corp	1959–64	JSM Hailey	1939–43
Simon Anderson	1983–7	Samuel Robert Alan Cox	2008–	John Haines	1944–9
John Apthorp OBE	1949–53	Victoria Helena Cox	2009–11	David CL Handcock	1976–80
James Arnold	2010–	RFH Crabb	1957–61	John E Handcock CVO DL	1944–7
Kyle Arnold	2009–	John D Crawley	1955–9	Robert Harland	1958–62
Zoe Arnold	2008–	Robert Curati-Alasonatti	2003–	Tim Harper	1978–83
Samuel Aron	2009–	Aronnan Dadral	2009–	Daisy Hart	2009–
Jan Ash	2003–9	Neil Davies	1986–9	Molly Hart	2009–
Thomas Patrick Atkinson		Vincent Davies		JJI Hawkins	1949–52
Jack Richard Baker	2003–10	Eric E de Garston	1940–4	Ethan Samuel Hayes	2005–
Sue Barnard	1956–91	Sachin Dhokia	2010–	Colin Hayfield	
Anthony Barrell	1961–6	AJ Dickinson	1947–52	Alastair Heald	2008–
Timothy Barrett	1955–60	Harvey Dodd	2008–	JM Helder	1945–50
Trevor Barton	1971–5	Miranda Dodd	2008–	RG Hill	1941–4
Christopher Beale OBE	1953–8	Rory Dodd	2008–	Michael Hirst	1946–50
Anthony M Bearman	1956–9	Peter George Dormon	1959–63	Mrs Janet Houghton	1986–
Raymond DR Berry	1949–54	Chris Draper	1957–62	Margaret F Howard	
Sir Michael Bett CBE	1948–53	Neil Durden-Smith OBE	1947–51	Christopher R Hudson	2007–
Oliver Beyrich	2008–	Howard Dymock	1989–2002	James W Hudson	2003–8
AJ (Tony) Bingham	1963–7	Ian Eggleden	1958–63	Matthew T Hudson	2005–10
Mike Bishop	1964–9	Alexander Evelegh	2005–	Anthony N Hunt	1949–54
Cedric B Blacker	1959–64	Camilla Evelegh	2005–	Mackenzie Hunt	2010
Marcus W Blake	1951–6	Carl E Failmezger	1982–3	Ray Hurrell	1965–70
Richard JB Blake	1949–53	Andy Fennell	1978–82	Kenan Huseyin	2009–
Adam Bloom	2004–9	Cameron Fennell	2004–8	David Jackson	1966–71
Ryan Bloom	2006–	Katherine Fennell	2005–7	Sheryar Jahangir	1984–7
Nigel Bonard	1960–4	Martin Field	1989–2005	James CN James-Crook	1968–72
Edred Nigel Bowman	1948–52	TA Ford	1979–	Martin A Jeens	1956–61
Lawrence Brewer	1959–64	Keith Fowler	1947–52	JC Joel	1946–51
The Brookwood Partnership Ltd		James Fowler	2006–	Deepak Johar	1974–9
Dr CR Brown	1946–51	Mr and Mrs N Frost		Andrew David Johnson	1970–5
Derick Burlingham-Johnson	1939–41	Tekin Fuad	1974–8	Piers Johnson	1983–8
WS Cairns	1962–7	Geoffrey Furber	1970–4	MR Jordan	1981–6
Peter AE Carr	1954–8	Austin Galvin	1970–2006	Christopher J Kershaw	1948–53
Matthew John Casey	1983–7	WH Gamble	1952–5	Frederikke Kistrup Strand	2009–
Matheus Cavalheiro	2009–	JH Gardner	1953–8	Simon Kitchen	1968–73
Lydia Chapman	2010–	Vicki Garson	2010–	Samuel Klein	2005–8
Howard Cloke	1974–9	Anya Gibbins	2009–	Richard I Knight	1975–80
Matthew Cobham	1985–9	Jack Gibbins	2007–	Dr Bertram Kueppers	1980
Gavin Cochrane	1946–50	David AK Gibson	1947–50	Bob Labes	1981–2
JJR Cockburn	1957–61	John Gillman	1969–73	Tim Law	1945–51
Matthew Remick Colleran	1974–7	Joe and Alison Godfrey		PW Leach-Lewis	1951–5
Marc Collier	2001–8	Olly RB Goodwin	2009–11	PK Leaver	1953–8
Wills Collier	2003–10	Judith Graham	1974–96	Peter Leaver QC	1958–63
Daniel Collins	1997–2002	Dr RHE Grant	1946–50	Weng Seng Leong	1975–80
Georgia Collins	2003–5	Guy Green	1971–3	Richard Graeme Levin	1973–8
Harry Collins	2006–11	PS Green	2005–	Andrew David Russell Lewis	1960–4
John R Collis	1951–6	Kevin M Greene	1958–63	Victoria Lindsey (née Hopkirk)	1982–4
John M Colvin	1952–6	Corrina Griffin	1988–90	Ian G Luetchford	1948–51

John MacLeod	1944–8	Sara Price	1987–2006	Jason Theodorou	2009–
H Basil Maddox	1951–6	Harry Pugh	1966–73	Sarvesh Thiruchelvam	2010–
Mirzan Mahathir	1972–7	Graham Pulsford	1971–5	L Brian Thomas	1948–52
David Male CBE	1942–7	Peter Purton OBE	1946–51	Stephen Christopher Thomas	1967–70
Idroos Markar	1974–9	Matthew Ralph	2007–	Hewlett Thompson	1942–7
David Marks	1965–9	David A Randall	1961–6	Rupert Philip Thornton	1998–2005
Stephen Martin		Christopher Raper	1972–7	Richard Thwaites	1944–9
James Oliver Massing	2002–9	David Read	1969–73	Tim Tight	1984–9
John McAllister	1967–2005	Derek Redmayne	1945–50	Nigel J Tottman	1975–9
Paul McCarty	1987–92	Frederick Reed	1991–4	Charles Tubbs	1969–73
Aidan McDonagh	2009–	Andrew W Reid	1980–5	AG Turner	1952–7
Angus McLaren	1935–8	Tim Reid	1993–2000	John A Turner	1973–7
Michael McNeill	1955–60	John C Richards Jr	1961–5	Cyril Tyson	1952–87
David Mead	1982–2010	RY Richards	1963–8	Ali Unal	2007–
Deborah Meadows	1980–5	JP Richfield	1975–80	Bahar Uttam	1958–61
JA Mence	1935–8	PG Richfield	1945–9	George Uttley	2007–
Elizabeth Merrick		PL Richfield	1977–82	Joanna Uttley	2008–10
Bethany Michel	2010–	Michael Gerrans Ridpath	1940–4	Mark Uttley	2000–7
Edward Middleton	1962–6	John David Rimer	1956–60	Simon Varrall	1965–9
Takuho Miki	2005–7	Callum Ritchie	2007–11	Field Marshal Lord Vincent	
Tobias Milfull	2007–	Tom Ritchie	2003–8	GBE KCB DSO	1945–50
John Martin Miller	1971–6	Matthew Rivers	1971–6	Rahul Vyas	2003–8
Alex Milligan	2007–	CDM Roberts MBE	1953–8	Renu Vyas	2006–9
Chris Milligan	2007–	Humphrey RM Roberts	1945–50	Alex Waldron	2008–
Hanif Moledina	1982–7	John Whitby Roberts	1952–5	Mrs David Wallace-Hadrill	1950–5 & 1962–86
Andrew Moss		The Rodger Family		Justin Ward	1957–60
Jacob Moss	2010–	Francis Rogers	1953–8	John (Jack) Armitage Waterfield	1949–51
Michael Newfield	1980–4	Graham Gordon Roots	1949–54	Mr and Mrs S Watkins	
Evangeline Noorali	2008–	Michael Rowe	1952–7	AL Waugh	1930–2
Yoel Noorali	2003–10	RA Rushton	1960–3	Max Weil	2010–
Edward Oatley MBE	1958–62	Richard Schooley	1963–8	David Penry Wicks	1965–70
Simon K Osborne	1961–6	Peter G Scott	1959–64	Robert A H Wildmore	1967–72
Michael Ost	1951–5	AJ Scott Knight	1954–9	Scott Wilson	2011–
Anthony John Owen	1948–52	CJM Searle	1964–9	Thomas Michael Stow Winfield	1944–7
Henry Padwick	1955–60	Thomas NH Selbey	1956–9	PJL Wingfield	1952–5
T Michael Palmer	1936–40	Carey Sheehan	1983–5	Simon Wolmark	1986–90
Ian Partington	1952–5	James Sheridan-Vigor	2006–11	Major Antony Wood TD	1954–9
Mrs Robert Bruce Partridge II	1957–8	Denis Shutin	2008–10	Caroline Woodrow	1984–6
Jayesh Patel	1985–7	Jonathan Simon ONZM	1963–7	Sarah Jane Woodrow	1982–4
Geoff Peach	1973–7	Paul FS Spencer	1943–7	Alex Worsley	2006–
Richard Peart	1955–60	Simon St Leger-Harris	1968–73	Elliott Worsley	2006–
Stephen DL Perry	1968–71	Robert Stokes	1949–83	Michael Wright	2000–7
Gary Philip	1983–8	James Stowell	2007–	Robert Wright	1960–5
CR Pianca	1960–4	Neil Sutherland OBE	1966–70	Roger Wright	1970–4
Andrew Pike	1959–64	Hashim Syed	2009–	Stephen Wright	2005–
David Pilcher	1950–5	Juhi Tailor	2010–	Marcus J Wurtz	1975–80
Michael Powles	1969–74	Sebastian Talbott-Haworth	2003–7	Paul Yule	1969–74
Geoffrey Prall	1936–40	Boon Sin Tan	1978–81	André David Zitcer	1974–7
Anthony Prax	2004–10	James A Tanner	1956–9		
Laurence Prax	2003–7	MJ Tapper	1949–53		
Jeffrey Prett		Michael Taylor CBE DL	1956–61		
Matthew Prett	2009–	Michael JG Taylor	1952–5		
Sophie Prett		David Peter Templeman	1995–8		

Index

This index is compiled on a word-by-word basis rather than letter-by-letter. Thus for example Black Watch precedes Blackburn. Major locations for an entry are printed in **bold.** Illustrative material and photographs are printed in *italics.*

Kennedy's House
and Martineau's House

Headmaster's House

Business Studies
Geography

Chapel

Headmaster
Bursar
Whitbread Room

Leeman's House
Riding's House

School Dining Hall

To Kennedy's House
and Martineau's House

Lib

Music School

Site of the new
Wells Centre

To Beevor's House
and McGill's House

Beevor's House

McGill's House